Our Comfort Zone

Our Comfort Zone

Alice White

Belleville, Ontario, Canada

Our Comfort Zone

Copyright © 2001, Alice J. White

All Scripture quotations unless otherwise specified are taken from the *New King James Version*. Copyright © 1979, 1980, 1982. Thomas Nelson Inc., Publishers.

Scriptures marked NIV are from *The Holy Bible, New International Version*. Copyright © 1973, 1978, 1984 International Bible Society. Used by permission of Zondervan Publishing House. All rights reserved.

ISBN: 1-55306-248-5

**For more information or
to order additional copies, please contact:**

Ms Alice Steward
1508 Switchgrass Rd
Edmond, OK 73013

, OK 73114

Essence Publishing is a Christian Book Publisher dedicated to furthering the work of Christ through the written word. *Guardian Books* is an imprint of *Essence Publishing*. For more information, contact:
44 Moira Street West, Belleville, Ontario, Canada K8P 1S3.
Phone: 1-800-238-6376. Fax: (613) 962-3055.
E-mail: info@essencegroup.com
Internet: www.essencegroup.com

Printed in Canada
by

To my Heavenly Father,
His Son, and the Holy Spirit—
because Christ lives in me,
I can do all things through Him;

and

to my family
who has contributed an important part
in the writing of Our Comfort Zone!

I wish to thank
Dr.'s Robert and Mary Anne McCaffree, M.D.,
the Brooks, and the Banowetzs
for their loving support
and for serving as role models.
Also,
Matthew and Belinda Walden
for their assistance
with this project.

Table of Contents

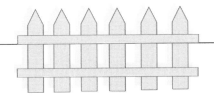

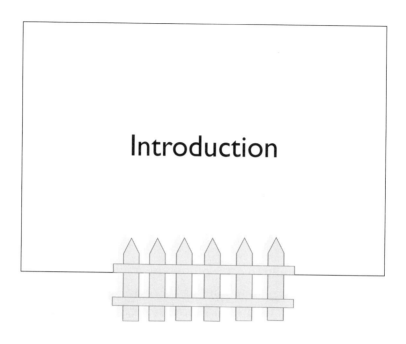

Introduction

M Y NAME IS ALICE WHITE and I am a fifty-four-year-old mother of three. I am writing this book so that my story may be of help to others when it seem like there is no way out. It is particularly geared to those having problems adjusting to life without the aid of AFDC, or struggling with other disadvantages life has brought their way. With all the policy changes regarding who can receive assistance and who can't, being forced to enter the working world is a big step out of one's comfort zone, especially for those who have small children.

I hope my story will encourage many women and men not to give up and will offer them the strength they need to have confidence. People can easily be motivated by the realization that they can make it on a small amount of money, and that, with their own self-esteem and relying on God as sole provider, they do not need to depend on assistance from the government or from any other source.

I myself was a mother of small children, receiving AFDC, afraid of working a minimum-wage job, not knowing if I was able to live up to everyone's expectations. If I didn't, I would be without an income to provide for the needs of my children. They were ages two, seven, and sixteen with no father figure around.

I had tried working several jobs, but it just didn't seem like they were going to cover our needs. While I was on assistance I had low income housing at about twenty dollars a month, as well as food stamps, free medical care, and a supplement check each month. It was our security blanket. I knew we would have a roof over our heads and food in our mouths from month to month if I obeyed the rules. But one day I decided I'd had enough; I wanted to live where I chose to, not where low-income housing dictated. I felt very poorly about myself but knew I wanted more out of life even though I didn't know where to start. In 1981 I decided to terminate my AFDC because I wanted more for my life and for my children. Our security blanket was removed.

It was a scary situation—hard to explain. You would have to live it in order to understand how such a situation makes a person feel. When you leave your comfort zone and go to a life that is completely new, anything can happen. However, never wanting to look back, we looked forward to the day we could find comfort in ourselves. I thank God for His grace and mercy upon us because we certainly needed it.

I was not a Christian at that time, but I knew God existed. I put my trust in Him and, although I was still afraid we might return to our old security blanket, we never did. We made it together with God in our midst.

Chapter One

A Troubled Teen Seeking Refuge

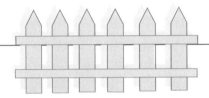

MY LIFE AS A CHILD WAS HARD. I came from a family that did not center on Christ and in which He was not loved. Our father was not there for us; he spent most of his life confined in prison. My mother was not able to cope with the situation and turned her life over to Satan, drinking every day. She could not perform without a husband to help raise the children. I guess we became a hardship for her instead of a blessing.

We heard about Christ at an early age but really didn't know what He meant in our lives. Christ was often spoken of in other family member's homes and I would attend services on occasion, even becoming baptized at an early age although I didn't really understand what it was about.

My family wasn't the storybook type with the white picket fence and parents that read their children bedtime stories, caressing them before they fell asleep. My mother started out with problems that were not solved before having children of her own; she too came from a dysfunctional family. A person raised in a dysfunctional family will very likely carry dysfunction into his or her own family if healing does not occur. My mother was very unhappy and did not know what to do. She did not seek God for an answer to her problems but began to look for answers in alcohol. Her self-esteem was low and she was lost. She was not able to give love and respect to her children or herself. Blinded by the enemy she did not know which route to take to end these problems.

We, her children, suffered and became dysfunctional people. The only life we knew was the one our parents modeled. My mother did not always behave badly; she tried to be a good provider in some ways but her dependency was on man, not God. Because she was depressed by our father's absence, she became very abusive. I was the oldest of seven, so I became the mother. I was only a child myself and never really experienced the fullness of girlhood and the joy of entering adulthood. I have always had the responsibilities of an adult. I had to cook for and clothe my siblings as if they were my children. Many days I was not permitted to play outside without them; they were always near me. I had to protect them from our mom when she was under the influence of alcohol. I was the one who made sure there was food on the table and clean clothes to wear. I was in bondage from an early age, trying desperately to find freedom. When my siblings got in trouble, I received the punishment. The stress was too much to carry on such small shoulders. To whom could I turn? What was the solution to my problems?

My youth was taken away and I was given the burden of an adult. We spent a lot of our days cooped up in the house while our mom was drinking. She felt that was the safest place for us, locked up like animals while others children were outside playing. One by one each of my siblings began to reach adolescence and drifted off to a life of problems.

I do believe my mother tried her best. When she was sober she was a good provider and mother, but while drinking, her personality changed. We were often afraid of her violent nature because we did not know what she might do to us. Sometimes we had to run for our lives as if we were the prey and she, the hunter. That's where my role of protector came in; I had to make sure no harm came to any of us.

When a problem arose from any of the children, I would be the one who paid the price—and what a big price to pay. We had no one to come to our rescue. There were an uncle and aunt who wanted to deliver us but they were afraid of my mother and her violent behavior. They hoped the problem would go away if they closed their eyes to the situation. Today, when the Department of Human Services finds out about neglect or abuse to children, they step in. The system was a failure to the children of my era. Oh, how my little heart would ache; it was so heavy with sorrow and I did not know what to do. Couldn't someone see our hurt? Why didn't someone help us?

Our father could have saved us, but he continued his abandonment. He was very sweet to us, but somewhere in his life he went the wrong way. He was raised by two Christian parents but even having a two-parent family was not the answer for him. Maybe he associated himself with the wrong people—I don't know.

The suffering we encountered made it hard for us to know how to love others or ourselves. I was afraid of love because I thought it would hurt. It brings tears to my eyes to think about my life as a child. I can't remember a lot of my childhood; it was so terrible, I suppressed it. Sometimes I wished I could die and end all the pain, but then I thought about my siblings. I had to be there for them. Finally, when I did break free, I felt as guilty for abandoning my siblings as a mother would feel if she abandoned her children.

I would pray but didn't know if God would hear the prayer of a little one. I guess He did, because He brought me out and my heart is beating even stronger. I thank God for having mercy on us. I prayed for death and He gave me an abundant life forever with Jesus.

When I was about fifteen, I had a vision. God showed me where I would one day serve Him. I remember telling my grandmother about the vision and she told me I had been bad and that was the reason for the dream. I have never forgotten it, and even to this day I can see it as vividly as that first night. I went to live with my grandmother seeking refuge from the terrible childhood I had experienced. I guess I felt like God had taken me out of a bad situation so I would be able to hear what He wanted me to hear. It was there I learned more about the Savior and I was able to complete my education. I was the only child of the seven in my family to complete high school. God will make a way for you, especially if He has called you into His service. No circumstances will stop the work of God.

The way the story began is this. I went to visit my grandmother in Arkansas at the age of fifteen, tired and run down, lost and feeling unwanted, depressed and a nervous wreck. When the time came for me to return home after my summer break, my mother came to get her babysitter but God stood in the way. He was good to me. Hidden in the dirty clothes bin outdoors, I was stored away for the use of the Lord so that my mother would not be able to take me back. I was so completely exhausted, I needed a way out, I needed refuge. Most of all, I needed someone to help me find myself and some happiness, someone to love me.

I tried, in all ways, to be model child, seeking respect from everyone, not getting into trouble or doing the things that kids do when they come from a dysfunctional family.

God had my life planned from my mother's womb. He planned to use me to help others and gave me the helper's heart I needed. Almost all of my sisters and brothers have had run-ins with the law, but not me. It was God that kept me away from that life, holding on to me for His purposes. I did not know or understand what an awesome God was leading and guiding me, molding me into who He wanted me to be.

As a child I could sense that I was a little different from other children my age. Some people would say I acted like a grown-up. I guess this was because I sought out the company of older people so I could continue to hear about Jesus. At that age I didn't realize why I wanted to be in their presence. I really didn't like being with other children because I didn't have the clothing and the other things they had. I was like an outcast and was made fun of which made me ashamed. Moreover, my heart was already hurting because of the abusive life I was living. No one really knew but my immediate family with whom I had sought refuge. I was too ashamed to let most people know I had come from parents that did not value their children. I never remember my mother coming to any of our school activities although we weren't involved in too many. Don't get me wrong; my mother wasn't a sex offender and she didn't torture us, she was just not a loving parent and sometimes very physical and mentally abusive. She needed Christ, but the enemy kept her blinded from the truth and she could not find her way out of bondage. My life with my grandmother was not as wonderful as I thought it was going to be, but I found more peace there. She was not able to buy me shoes, clothing, or other things young girls like. I never had my own bedroom, but maybe that was a good thing. I learned, at an early age, to share.

My grandmother lived a Christian life to the best of her ability, and she attended church on a regular basis. I went along to learn about Christ and all I heard stayed with me. Although I never strayed completely away from what I was taught, I didn't live the life. I learned how to survive at an early age and decided that one day I was going to be respectful. I didn't know how I was going to master this, but deep inside my soul I had the spirit of God leading, directing, and showing me what He wanted me to do.

The Heavenly Father had planned a life I knew nothing about. Joseph's brothers cast him into a pit because they disliked him, and then sold him into slavery, but God held him close to His heart. Joseph became a provider for his family, a way out of famine. I thank God for holding onto me and providing light to my siblings through me. He was molding me into what he wanted me to be.

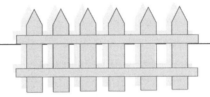

Chapter Two

School Away from Home

AFTER I DECIDED TO LIVE WITH my grandmother, I began to attend a school name Childress High in Nashville, Arkansas. It was about a thirty-minute drive from Dierks, the small town in which I was living. Each morning I had to ride the bus to school. I concentrated on my lessons and made friends with a few girls in my social class that could be trusted not to make me feel ashamed of my appearance. I had no money to spend like other children, but that wasn't anything new. Coping was normal for me, something I was very good at.

My grandmother had a daughter about my age named Wilma Sue. We went to the same school which made things a little easier. She became my sister in many ways. We spent a lot of time playing and laughing together, doing things that were normal for girls our age. She was a better student than I which challenged me to achieve better grades. I did not participate in many activities because of my finances but was able to join the school drill team. I loved to dance and learned the moves so well I was made the team leader. That made me feel better about myself, and other people began to pay more attention to my existence. My very closest friends were Joann Wesson, Curlie Simmons, Vertise F. Brown. They were my hearts without whom I would not have been able to make it through school. We were so close, we started a club named "The Four Aces" and felt like it was the neatest.

My teachers liked me and felt sorry for me. One of them told me that when you are happy, the world smiles with you, but when you are sad, you are sad alone. I remembered that and tried never to let anyone know my inner feelings. That's partly the reason for my mixed-up life. I used that saying against myself when I should have used good judgment; there are some things you should talk about and some you shouldn't.

I hardly had enough money to buy lunch, so I brought sack lunches. One day I went to the cafeteria and asked if I could work for my lunch. I was hired on the spot. This pleased me as I had often smelled the aroma from the cafeteria, and eating a hot lunch seemed so much better than a cold sandwich. This was another step up in my life. I learned to work with other students as well as faculty.

I was not very outgoing because I was afraid someone would find out about my past. It was better to limit those with whom I associated. I studied hard so I could graduate with honors. As graduation approached, I did not have the money to buy my class ring or my prom dress. I got a job working in the field chopping cotton, something a city girl didn't know much about. They gave me a chance but I was fired the first day. At least I tried. Still needing another job I went and did something a little more simple; I picked pecans and cucumbers and made enough money to buy my gown and ring.

Around prom time our school was having a talent show. I was trying to fit in with the others girls, so when they decided to enter the talent show, I thought, *Oh! I can sing pretty well.* I entered. I practiced my song every day and felt confident I was ready to compete. When I walked on stage before all those people, I froze. I couldn't remember but two or three words of my long-rehearsed song. That became another lesson learned: never try and follow in someone else's footsteps. Never be anyone but yourself.

Eventually the time came and I graduated from high school a B-average student, very proud to wear my cap and gown. I'd worked hard for my diploma and was sorry I did not have the finances to go to college. However, finishing high school was difficult enough; I was not ready for another challenge.

Children raised in dysfunctional homes can be like animals in a jungle. They fight among themselves not having learned love and respect or proper behavior. Dysfunctional children do not have identities or direction—they are lost. God has placed parents over families to teach children His laws. Without those guidelines lives go in all kinds of negative directions. With the guidance of God, you are sure to do right thing to yourself and others. We might stray away but eventually the Holy Spirit will bring us back to God, face to face. Building a relationship with God was what I needed but I didn't know how. Maybe it just wasn't the right time.

Chapter Three

Back to My Beginning

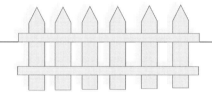

AFTER GRADUATION I DIDN'T WASTE much time going back to my roots. I hadn't seen my family in a while and missed them. Now that I was grown I didn't have to live with my mother. It was good to be back but my siblings were scattered like sheep. Some were in situations from which they couldn't escape and some did not want to escape. I felt guilty that I had abandoned them and responsible for their scattering. I went to live with relatives until I was able to make it on my own by working domestic jobs with low wages. I was surviving.

I met this guy, Melvin White, whom I later married. It was a bad relationship and marriage. I finally decided I wanted no more of his abuse and ended the relationship though not the marriage. I decided that if I was going to have it rough, I might as well have it by myself. I now had three children to raise and no husband to help. My life was like a carousel going round and round with no complete stops. I was searching for something, feeling lost and blind, betrayed by my mother and by the man I thought loved me. I was looking for answers in the wrong places, getting no responses. Something was missing but I couldn't stand still long enough to find out. At this time I was known as a square; I didn't smoke nor drink—a saint without the halo.

Later I began to do what everyone else does when the pain of life is upon them and they do not have God. I traded in my sainthood, conducting myself in the manner of my peers, forgetting all about God and deciding to carry the trials of life on my own shoulders. God had something waiting for me but I didn't know when and where I would receive it. Still, the day of His deliverance would come.

Life had to go on, even for a young person who had experienced so much difficulty. Although life is not a storybook and we all have problems, we need to find the answer to the question, "What Would Jesus Do," in all situations! This is easy to say, but when you are faced with a problem you must have the Spirit of the Lord to bring you through. You might fall several times, but God will be there to help pick you up. He gives us all choices and won't go force us beyond our will. If we desire to get up He'll be there to raise us out of any situation. He raised Christ from the grave. Is there anything impossible for God? He *is* the impossible! Having faith is hard but if you work on it day by day it becomes stronger and stronger. There is not a mountain in your life that cannot be removed by faith in God. Faith is powerful; the more you have and the more you use it, the stronger it gets.

Abraham was a man of faith and was blessed because of it. In Genesis 12:14, Abraham received a specific call from God to leave his homeland and go to the land of Canaan. Through faith and obedience he became the father of many nations (Genesis 17:5). When he found himself at an old age without an heir, God blessed him with a son because of his faith. The faith of Abraham was also dramatically tested (Genesis 22:1). He was commanded by God to give his only son as a burnt offering. Abraham obeyed and was about to slay his son when God stopped him. Abraham's faith and commitment to God were proven and God again promised to make a blessed nation of his descendants (Genesis 22:18). God blessed the life of Abraham in every way (Genesis 24:1).

Job was rich and respected, a righteous and religious man. He was the least likely candidate to be inflicted with calamity. But Satan is the accuser of God's people (Revelation 12:10), and his sneering attack on Job prompted God's providential permission of Job's suffering (Job 1:2). Job lost his sons, daughters, his sheep, herds, and his servants. Finally he lost his health. Still, Job retained his faith and declared, *"The Lord gave, and the Lord has taken away: blessed be the name of the Lord"* (chapter 3). Even though Job went so far as to curse the day he was born, it is important to remember that he never lost his faith and never cursed God.

Not all our suffering is the result of sin. Job was a righteous man who feared God (chapter 42). In the end he was lavishly rewarded. God gave Job double the possessions he had in the beginning. God gave him as many children as he had to begin with. The Lord blessed the latter days of Job more than the earlier (Job 42:12). However, more precious than any other reward given to Job was the reward of a crown of life. God gave Job a life crowned with the perfection that comes only through patient suffering (James 1:12).

Followers of Christ will go through rocky situations; the road is not always smooth. God gives us authority over our lives through Christ Jesus. Faith has been around for a long time. If it worked for the patriarchs of the Bible, it will continue to work for us and with more power because of the blood of Jesus and the promise of eternal life in Him.

I was a single parent, but I did not completely fall apart like my parents. I was not a very affectionate mother, but I did make all provisions I could to raise my children the way I thought was right. God was there with me all the time. I did not want to my children to be scattered everywhere like my family was. Even though I was lonely and needed a good husband, I could not find one. My marriage had been all wrong from the beginning. I married someone that Satan had shackled, blinded, and did not want free. There was too much wrong in the relationship to even try to straighten out. Sometimes you have to turn a person over to his or her desires and go on. I needed a Christian husband that would be appropriate in the company of my children and I was not going to settle for just anyone. I had seen the pattern of my mother. Why live a terrible life and take my children down the same path? Raising children by myself was hard, but I kept a roof over their heads and food on the table by cleaning houses and by Aid for Dependent Children which was our security blanket. I was afraid to stop receiving AFDC because the jobs I worked only paid minimum wage without many benefits. I knew that if I received assistance each month I would get my check, my children and I would be fed, and our medical expenses would be paid. I did not want to continue to receive benefits from the government because, to me, it was something to be ashamed of. But what could I do?

I did not know which way to turn. I started hanging around the wrong crowd which led to smoking marijuana, drinking alcohol, and sometimes taking pills. My heart was heavy and burdened and I could not believe my childhood problems were suddenly magnified. My heart constantly cried, *Please someone help me, show me what is going on in my life!* That was where the drugs came into play: not knowing whether any day was my last or whether there would be more to come. I pleaded, *If someone out there has the answer, please let me know how to get free and let me raise my children the way they should be raised. I don't know what tomorrow may bring. If there is an answer somewhere, how can I find it? I am so tired. I have tried my best and not profited from it. I went through hell as a child and now as an adult I am still in hell! When will I finally be let loose? I am seeking help but no one hears me. But then, I am not asking where someone can hear me. I don't know how to start asking for help. Whom can I trust? I am in my own prison serving time for I don't know how long and I don't understand why. I am a good person; I went to school and completed it. I was not an A-student, but I was average and with the problems I had, how did I make it? I didn't steal, kill, and I wasn't abusive. I tried to love everyone so that love would be returned. If I could find an answer, I would be released from the prison within myself. Help me somebody!*

I sent my children to school dressed appropriately and taught them what I thought they needed to know. I didn't leave them with just anyone, running off trying to find myself. My children knew I was not the sweetest mom in the world, but I did the best I could. I would smoke marijuana to help me cope, to help me give my children the attention they needed.

I often asked, *Who am I?* I needed to find my identity before I could break the bars around my life. I knew my name was Alice but who was she? What purpose did she have in the world? I had to reach her and find out if there was a place for her. Finding yourself is the first step in breaking free; it is the price you pay for freedom. I had to try harder to find myself, not just for me but for the children I brought into the world.

So now let me get started. Finally, there was a beginning, a place to start. I could begin to breathe even though my heart was so heavy and my life was so hollow and meaning-less and unhappy. I knew there must be more to life than heartache and pain. I could see smiles on people's faces, birds flying, green trees and grass, and I knew God made all of this for a reason. I knew He did not mean for anyone to be unhappy and that there is no other way but to pick up our beds and walk. He tells us through creation to reach out and touch the hem of His garment. There is not a jail nor situa-tion He cannot deliver you from. Faith will free you! Thank you Jesus!

Without Christ there is no good life, no firm foundation. He will hold you and you will always be left standing. (I know because I am one of the blessed.) This is not something I got from a book; it is my living testimony of what God will do if you let Him into your heart.

He is not a hurry-up-and-fix-it God; He comes in His own time but He is always on time. I tried all my ways and it was time to try God's ways. What did I have to lose? Drugs and men didn't make me happy so there could only be one way out. No shining armor was going to save me, only the blessed grace of God giving me strength.

When I was younger I thought that if I accepted Christ as my savior I would be missing something in the world. I found out that everything I needed was in Christ. This was the only way to survive; without Him I would only see destruction. I didn't want that. There had been enough destruction in my life. So I prayed. *Have mercy! I am crying out to you because I know you will not betray me. I am coming to you Lord to find salvation in your Son. I know there is peace in you and I can see the sun shining bright in Christ. The glorious hour of my salvation is here—take me Lord and use me as you see fit. I am nothing but filthy rags begging you to cleanse me and set me free. My heart is pounding and I feel the bars breaking. I see a new life coming my way. I love you, Jesus. Stay with me and never leave me. I see a brighter tomorrow. I see life and happiness before me. I can see now who Alice is, where she is going, and who will take her. My Jesus, my Jesus!*

If I had reached out and surrendered my life before I would not have been imprisoned so long. I would not have been shackled or blinded by the world and it's contents. I would not have needed drugs or any other worldly vices to help me exist. I suddenly knew that what He had done for others He would do for me.

However, after accepting Christ as my savior I slipped and fell again into the worldly activities of the ungodly ones. I left my first love. But even though I forgot what I had learned, this time I knew who I was. That gave me an advantage. I knew right from wrong like Adam and Eve but, like them, was tempted and fell. At the time it felt good. I decided to try it on my own one more time, because God was taking too long. I thought I needed to help Him find me some happiness. Remember Abraham and Sarah? They, too, tried to help God and messed up.

I knew that whatever happened, God was still there with me. That gave me strength. Knowing right from wrong, my eyes were open so who could I blame this time when trials came upon me? I wanted to rush happiness now that I had Christian values and not wait on God. I knew there was a good husband for me and I guess I wanted to take the credit for finding him, wanted to say I did it by myself and not even the Father helped me. Another big mistake! I started looking in the wrong places without realizing I was already in the right place to find a good husband—the church. Blinded again, I wound up right back where I started.

I was beginning to become depressed with life again and depressed that I'd put God back on the shelf. It was taking a toll on my health. *Why am I doing this to myself when I have children that need me?* I thought. I began to purposely concentrate on my health and children, to hang up the pity party because it was not going to help me. That is the way the enemy attacks; he knocks you down and stomps until you cannot get up. I was ashamed to call on God because of the sins I'd committed. I knew He saw everything. How dared I sin and boldly go to Him when trouble came? Was I to stay in the camp of the enemy or should I go back to God and ask for forgiveness? It is a hard decision to make when you have turned your back on the only one who truly loves you. But life and death were set before me and God wouldn't help with the decision. He left it all up to me. No man knows the day nor the hour that our savior will return. I didn't want Him to come back before I gave Him back my life. Never put off for tomorrow what you can do today.

If salvation is at the tip of your tongue, Christ is waiting. He knows our weakness and died for our sins so that we could have eternal life, just for the asking.

And God will wipe away every tear from their eyes; there shall be no more death, nor sorrow, nor crying. There shall there be no more pain, for the former things have passed away (Revelation 21:4).

This was the chance for me to have what I didn't receive in this life and more. But the question in the back of my mind rang out, *Are you ready?*

Why am I so blinded? I know this is my chance? Why am I not reaching toward our higher power? Where is my willpower? The enemy is putting obstacles in front of me. Here I go again, my yoyo life. I should be tired, but I'm still fighting and not laying totally down: kind of dragging and trying to serve two masters: God and the enemy. How is this going to work? I know it is not right, but the Holy Spirit is talking to me and I am trying to listen. This might be my last chance. I am playing around with my life and the life of my children. Why would the Father help me when I haven't done anything for Him but call on His name when I was in trouble? Will He respond? I don't know.

You can't trust Satan even if you are very obedient to his call. You can do all he requires and he will turn his back on you when you least expect. God will try to get through to us as we pray, but we have to listen quietly as He speaks. We need to pray for wisdom and ask God to turn our sorrow into hope as we place our emotions in His hand. God will deliver each of us from eternal tragedy and the present evil of this world. He allows us to take risks, yet the power of His deliverance is available to us when we fall. Accepting the Bible's view of God can give us courage in stressful times. The Holy Spirit led the prophets and other Bible writers to see God as the supreme being and judge of the earth. No matter how bad things might appear, how hopeless the situation, God will triumph over evil and vindicate those who trust Him. The whole Bible declares that message; it counteracts the mood of hopelessness that too many people suffer from in our day. Beginning with Genesis, the Bible portrays a God in control of His universe. The resurrection of Christ was the climactic evidence of God's victory over evil and death. So don't give up; you are something in the eyes of God. I know without Christ I am in the battle alone—warfare with no armor, no helmet, nothing against the enemy. I can hold out a little while, but it won't be long before he tramples me down. With Christ I have a great defender.

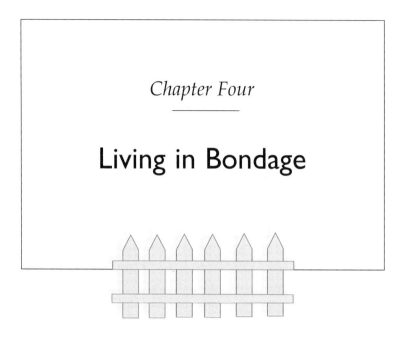

Chapter Four

Living in Bondage

I WAS STILL DEPENDING ON AFDC and cleaning houses on occasion. When I had strength to find work it would add to my depression. The heart of it was that welfare felt degrading as I had my health and strength and could work. It would have been another story if I needed assistance because I couldn't work or had bad health or too many small children to look after. I believe it is appropriate for some people, but it wasn't for me because I wanted more. I was ashamed to let certain classes of people know I was a recipient of government handouts. Each month, when I received my check and food stamps, I would deposit my check in my bank account, rush out a few days later when I felt like everyone else with stamps had finished shopping, and then spend all my stamps at once. In order to leave no evidence of my food stamps I would go to the stores in which it was most likely that other people spent stamps. The system dictated where to shop. Why couldn't I just accept my poverty level and go on?

Some people were cruel when they found out I received aid from the government. A doctor once asked, during a visit, if there were any doctors on the east side that could treat me. He was my choice and the government was paying him. I wasn't dirty nor did I have an odor and always dressed neatly. I was pleasant to talk to, so what was the problem? Did he forget the code of ethics? I wonder if he had been caught up in a world of color and felt I wasn't worth treating. Did he not know I was trapped in a situation I didn't want? People like him can scar a person forever. I will never forget how I felt, but I will forgive him and leave him to God. One must leave the judging to Him.

I went back to school again to be a medical transcriber and got a certificate. At that time the welfare system didn't make recipients go to school or find jobs, especially if they had small children. I did it on my own, trying to escape from my comfort zone. But after graduating, I didn't know where to find a job. Who would hire me? I needed a job that would provide for my family as I was all they had. I only wanted to earn a break in life—not a handout, but a "hand-up." The very reason I'd continued to live in my comfort zone was that I didn't want anything undeserved. Why did I work so hard to receive a degree in school? It was certainly not to continue to live in the shackles of my old security blanket, the comfort zone. I didn't need an education for that, only some dependents! Trying to escape the agony of being under the system,

I carried myself in such a way that many people didn't know I was receiving assistance. My children were well cared for, and my living conditions were nice and clean. We had always lived in public housing in order to pay low-income rent. Each apartment was nice and not run down, but I wanted to do better. I wanted to make my own decisions.

God was the way to begin my adventure in life, and self-pity was the way to destruction. I knew this because I was taught at an early age about God and what He can do. I saw it all around me yet didn't have the strength to call upon Him. Was I bringing destruction on myself? I would have been more able to cope with my circumstances if I'd had God in my life.

Chapter Five

A Brighter Tomorrow?

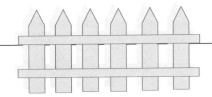

F INALLY THINGS WERE LOOKING GOOD for me, I thought! I had a lady working with me through rehabilitation, trying to help me better my situation. After receiving a certificate from American Transcriptions School, she located a position for me at a finance company. My position was Head Cashier, and I worked there almost two years. I wasn't earning a high wage, but it was a position that made me look and feel pretty good. I did struggle to make ends meet, because as soon as I was hired the security blanket I held so close dropped me like a hot potato. Wages were very low in 1978, as the economy was weak. I did not know if we would make it. Nevertheless, it was the end of my comfort zone at that time. I was happy to be in a position where I could meet people and be recognized as the girl who worked at the finance company. I still remained in low-income housing; the administrators helped subsidize my income and charged rent accordingly. I was able to buy clothing and all necessary items. I really liked my position and became efficient enough to take loan applications, check them out, and approve them or turn them down. I thought I was hot stuff!

The system didn't evaluate me to see if I had enough income to pay for my family's medical expenses. I left the comfort zone without a car and had to walk about three miles to work each day. I couldn't catch a ride or pay for a cab. I was trying to hold on to my life and not let go, because I was walking on thin ice. I didn't know when it would crack and I would fall through. The depression was still there, disguised by the smile on my face. I received a regular high for breakfast, lunch, and dinner. Staying high was the only way I could cope with the struggle. Still, depression was taking a toll on my body, and the partying and pot smoking were just as bad. I couldn't afford to seek medical help, besides which, I was ashamed to tell anyone that I had a problem. This went all the way back to my childhood when I felt lost in a world of darkness and distress that I couldn't identify or touch. It was a part of my life I did not want but could only free myself by trying to suppress it. In my ignorance I didn't know this was a demon that needed to be dealt with, brought to the surface, looked straight in the eye, and regarded as a problem.

One day trouble came and I had to let my position go. I needed some medical help and could not afford it. The system was determined to get me back, so they said they could not help me if I had a job. I could not afford this bill. When would it end? Where could I go from there? Was I to return to my old comfort zone—Aid for Dependent Children—and continue in a world of depression, that old scenario? Eventually, in order to get the medical help I needed, we went back to the security blanket.

Sometimes I felt if I ever found a way out it would be too late. I needed an escape route immediately but I kept dancing around the only way—Jesus Christ. Why did I keep torturing myself? Why didn't I let it all go and return to the peace and love of Christ? Our human nature is to be hard-headed, making life more complicated than it really is. I thought that one day, when I was really tired, I would give up, leave all my cares behind me, and let Christ take full control.

How long, Lord? Give me the strength to come and pick up my cross and follow you. I am wading in self pity and about to drown, but I am still swimming. Maybe one day I will get out of the water and come to Jesus, where I will find safety, security, and everlasting life.

My children don't really know what's going on in my life. I can't confide in them. I am ashamed to let them know that I have problems that I don't know how to deal with. I am trying to raise them the best I can despite my own problems. I am trying to make life easier for them than it was for me because I don't want them to suffer as I did. Maybe I don't show it, but they are all I have and I love them so much.

I just couldn't find the words to tell my children, so I thought I would show them by making sure they didn't suffer. I wanted to be the best mom to them, because my mother wasn't there for me. I wanted to turn the other way and show my mom how it should go and what she should have done as a parent.

Sometimes my mother acted envious of the way I was raising my children, keeping them wrapped in my security blanket. I let no harm or danger come their way; I was their shield in times of trouble. We were all together as a family and not scattered like wild animals. Children do not ask to be born but are here because of their parents. And even though I was not a perfect, affectionate mom, I made sure they had what they needed to survive. They didn't have to go around hungry or dirty and were better dressed than a lot of the children they played with.

When I wasn't able to buy new clothing, I would purchase it from a resale or garage sale and wash and press it so it would look really sharp. I always received compliments on how I cared for my children and paid attention to their manners. I was active in the Parent Teacher Association. My kids were good students which was one of my requirements. I never wanted them to end up in my situation. They were rarely absent because I didn't want them to miss a lesson and were not involved in many school activities because we couldn't afford it.

When they were small, my children didn't give me the problems many single-parent families experience. Even when they became teenagers they respected me and their peers. I demanded respect from my children just as my mother had from us. Even though she had faults, I really think she did the best she could. My mom needed strength to go on and maybe she was suffering from depression like me and didn't know what the problem was. The strength she found was the wrong kind—alcohol—and it took her life. I know today she has found peace with God. She was not a bad person, only lost within herself, crying out for help. No one could hear her, because the words would not come out of her mouth. I understand what is meant by a "generational curse." We had a curse on our family, but as of today, I am breaking it off. It's hard for a single parent to raise children alone, but it is even harder for two parents pulling in different directions. I was by myself, but I had to continue trying to do what was best for my children.

When my girls became teenagers, my oldest, Taunja, and my middle daughter, Connie, started giving me some problems. At the time I felt it was the worst thing they could do but have since spoken with other parents and many of their children made my girls look good. They were never really terrible. My daughter La'Donna gave me no trouble at all, although her mouth sometimes brought trouble on herself. I thank God for my three girls. None of them ever had an run-in with the law, they don't sell drugs, and are not alcoholics, so whatever problems they had could be worked out.

Chapter Six

Hard Times, New Outlook

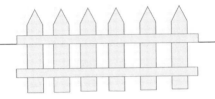

SOON I DECIDED TO JOIN CHURCH AGAIN—my second attempt to do the right thing. Yet I was still serving two masters, not really being faithful to God. I thought if I gave Him some of my time, my problems would vanish and I would find happiness. This was something I truly longed for as obstacles in my life had prevented it. I was active at church and attended every meeting so I could devote more time to God than to the world. But I still had not gained a relationship with Christ and did not know that I should. I thought by going to church, and taking my children with me, my responsibility was completed. My children were getting older and the enemy started using them against me. This was during the teenage years I spoke about earlier. My oldest daughter started to cause me great amount of heartache, I guess because I had planned her life out for her which was a mistake. I continued to pray and cried out to the Lord to help me. I wondered why there were so many problems in our life. Where did I go wrong? My prayers were not being answered as quickly as I wanted. God was working all the time on my behalf, I just couldn't see it. I wanted instant results. We continued serving God and learning more about His son, Jesus. We knew our dependence must be in the Lord. Our only lasting and guaranteed security was to trust Him. No disaster comes without God's knowledge and permission, *"And we know that all things God works for the good of those who love him, who have been called according to his purpose"* (Romans 8:28 NIV). That assurance is our true security. Jesus said:

> *I am the true vine, and my Father is the gardener.... Remain in me, and I will remain in you. No branch can bear fruit by itself; it must remain in the vine. Neither can you bear fruit unless you remain in me* (John 15:1,4 NIV).

Stay close to Jesus through prayer and the study of His Word. Trust Him to help you overcome every temptation to sin that might stand in the way and hinder you from bearing fruit for Him. Through the power of the resurrection you can put temptation to death, be obedient to God's will, and die to your physical cravings. We cannot do it on our own, but we can let God accomplish His purpose in our lives.

All believers have the indwelling, enlightening presence of the Holy Spirit to empower and direct them. This tremendous power in our inner spiritual being is one of the main weapons we have against Satan. We can strengthen our inner nature through submission and obedience to the Holy Spirit. Do not grieve the Spirit through ungodly living (Ephesians 4:30). Do not quench the Spirit (1 Thessalonians 5:19). Instead, by faith, acknowledge the presence of the Spirit in your life and follow Him (Romans 8:14). Allow Him to produce the fruit of Christ-likeness in your life (Galatians 5:22-23).

I was beginning to find peace in turning my back on some of the things of the world, but was still keeping company with unbelievers and maintaining bad habits. I was calling myself a Christian because of the fellowship I had with Christians but was still going to church and studying God's Word high, because I felt like I wouldn't make it without smoking pot. God wasn't really real to me because I hadn't yet formed a relationship with Him. I couldn't hear or see Him because I was still blinded by my past. I wasn't seeking the things of God, only pacifying myself until the hot water I had climbed out of cooled off.

Mother Murphy was the founder of our church. She loved the Lord and did all she could to teach each of us to live holy and godly lives without any blemishes. I held on for her sake, because I admired the relationship she had with God. I wanted to be continually in her presence to learn all I could about God and how I could be blessed like her. I was trying to please man instead of God, living continually in darkness, fooling only myself, and living a life of make-believe.

"…*Behold, the fear of the Lord, that is wisdom, And to depart from evil is understanding*" (Job 28:28). I didn't have fear of the Lord nor wisdom to shun evil. I only knew that my past life was what kept me going and I didn't know what else to do. Although I was being taught how to live a godly life, for some

41

reason I heard but could not grasp it. If I had only sought God's wisdom, He would have given me the power of the Holy Spirit to understand the things and the nature of God. Deep down I was really enjoying being lost, not wanting to change because I was still blinded by the things of the world. Satan had me exactly where he wanted me—lost in my own ignorance. If I had known who God really was, I could have broken the shackles off my life much sooner.

Chapter Seven

Running Away from Reality

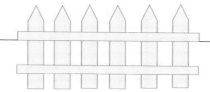

FINALLY ONE DAY I DECIDED to go back to the life I had said I was tired of. This was my second fall and I lived to regret it. I wish I had sought God instead of man so I wouldn't have cared what the church folk had to say. I was living my life based on what people thought about me. God gives us five senses with which to make our own decision and He does override them. As they say, "you made your own bed hard, now sleep in it." I was still living in the section-eight apartment, getting assistance and cleaning houses. I decided to try and better myself without God, because church just wasn't for me. Don't get me wrong, I never forgot the teaching about Jesus. When hard times came upon me, I knew how to call on the name of the Lord. I was out of church, but church was not out of my mind. God often came to me at the least expected times, reminding me of what I was taught. Deep in my heart I kept a place for Him and every day longed for something I couldn't define. Now I can; it was a closer walk with Jesus. He had touched me in some way and my life would never be the same. Even when I would be with friends getting high I would tell them about my Jesus and they would listen. Sometimes I didn't even want to get high because I was beginning to have a conscience which let me know it was wrong. I felt compassion for the ones that was not able to control their high, so God continued to use me even though I was dirty myself. Sometimes I would have a circle of people around me asking about the things of God. The times I sat and listened to Mother Murphy were not in vain. God was using me to wake up the spirit that dwelled in the ungodly.

Sometimes I wonder if this was God's plan to show me His marvellous ways, because I could hear my spoken words in my inner spirit and was able to learn about the goodness of God from my own mouth. During this period in my life, I began to hear some of the things God impressed upon me. One day, as I was looking out my bedroom window, I heard a voice say to me, "You are going to write a book and you will not be rich, but I will bless you." This happened some twenty years ago, but it never departed from my mind or my heart. I didn't know what I would write about, but I knew, when the time came, He would reveal it to me. Everyday I wanted a closer walk with God and I was learning.

Chapter Eight

A Brighter Tomorrow

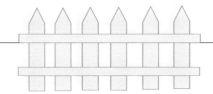

I DECIDED TO BETTER MY LIFE with new surroundings, so I enrolled in some classes at Oscar Rose Junior College, in 1979, to get a degree in business. I worked hard and was on the Vice President's Honor Roll. While I was there I began to do research on different fields of work and salaries. I found out that being an executive secretary, the field I was studying, was not going to free me from my comfort zone. I found out that if I had my own business in commercial and residential cleaning I could possibly turn in my old security blanket permanently. I knew how to clean since cleaning had been my supplemental income so I dropped out of school after three semesters to search for my freedom.

In 1981 I opened my own business, a commercial and residential cleaning service. I filed it at the County Court House under my name, which was the beginning of breaking free and becoming my own person. I had a verbal contract to clean the homes of three prominent families: Dr.'s Robert and Mary Anne McCaffree, Mr. John Brooks and his wife, Susan, and Dr. Mike Banowetz and his wife, Pauletta. They were the beginning of my search for identity. They often told other associates about my ability to clean and my trustworthiness. That helped a lot and I also ran advertisements in different papers or wherever I felt it would be noticed. Most of the time I had as many houses as I could clean by myself and sometimes more.

Susan Brooks was in real estate and I wanted somewhere to live on the northwest side where the crime rate was low and I could raise my children in a better environment and in better schools. I would take whatever I could afford, as long as it was decent. I spoke to Susan about my plan to move and she told me it would be better if I moved into something I planned on buying. I knew I could not get a home on my own with no credit references and had just started working. So the three families—the McCaffrees, the Brooks, and the Banowetzs—decided to help me break free from section-eight housing and made provisions for us to live in a house of our choice. One day I was called to look at a house on N.W. 82nd St.; it was in really poor condition. I didn't have to take it because there were three houses for me to look at. The three families came with me to view the property, and instantly I knew the picture was all wrong. As we walked through the rooms and saw their shabby condition, I began to cry. My family (which is what I call these people since our relationship went so far beyond work) thought I was crying tears of joy. In truth I was crying because God had whispered that this was my house. My spirit cried out to Him, saying, "Lord no! Please not this house! My section-eight apartment looks better than this." The Father said to me, "We can repair this place." But I said, " Lord, I have never done any of that kind of work before." He told me He would help me. No one heard this conversation of course, because my spirit had met the spirit of the Lord! This was a spiritual interaction with God almighty! I knew that if God would take time to talk to an unworthy vessel like me, I was willing to listen. I knew I should accept this house under any circumstances, obeying God and making a good choice. This would be a new beginning for my children and me. The Father said, "You have a lot of work to do, so roll up your sleeves and get started."

The house was not broken down with holes in the walls; it was just not cared for. It was filthy and roach infested, and the carpet looked like dogs had slept on it. It also had mice which I was afraid of. The color of the woodwork was terrible and painted with bad taste. It was an unimaginable array of colors with odors to match. It consisted of three bedrooms, two sitting rooms, two bathrooms, and a kitchen. There was also a tiny utility room in which I could squeeze a washer and dryer—acceptable and needed. The yard had no landscaping, front or back. The front was in poor condition, and the back was like a long-forgotten wilderness. The weeds and tree branches were so overgrown, they were taller than me and I am over five feet. I looked at all this and said, "Lord, I know you said to take on this job and I will obey. But you will have to show me what to do and how to do it." In the back there was a shed about to fall over. It was so full of unwanted, unusable junk that you could not walk in. This way my chance to get rid of my comfort zone and I took it. My family was happy for me though I don't really know what went through their minds when I said I would take it. They were proud and knew I could improve the condition of the house. Things had started to happen really fast. I started my business in July of 1981 and in September of the same year we got our home. I knew that God had not judged me for my actions, but by my heart. He heard my cry and knew I was tired and ready to serve. He was giving me some of the things I desired and the peace of mind that would enable me to serve Him.

My caseworker closed my case and told section eight to end my housing. She was very good to me, telling me to wait until my youngest child was in school. La'Donna was only two years old, and the system doesn't mind carrying you with children that small. I told her I had to go right away, but if I ever needed assistance I would come back. I never did. Sometimes my three girls and I did not know where our next meal would come from. I had the house payments as well as all the bills and essential things which totalled more than the income I was bringing home. I didn't know how to budget what I had.

My families recognized I was having problems making house payments, so they came up with a good plan. I would work for them and they would open an account for my house payments in their names. The house had always been in their names because I didn't have the credit to have it put in mine. Each time I worked for them the payments went directly into the bank account. That way my house would not be in jeopardy. I worked hard trying to stay afloat; I never asked for help even though I knew they would. That was the pride in me. I even hired different people to build up my clientele, so one day I wouldn't have to struggle so much by myself. Hiring employees never worked out. I continued to struggle to make ends meet, sometimes cleaning three houses in one day. I was my own boss and one of the best when it came to cleaning. I was able to set my own price, keeping it low so the big companies wouldn't underbid me. I even tried to specialize in cleaning beauty salons, but couldn't keep any help. My children started to help out when they were older, but they got tired. So I decided to give up on hiring someone and just keep the work I could handle by myself. Even though I was not in church, God was still in my heart and I knew if I did the right things, He would help me.

I continued to clean both commercial and residential places, making more money working than the system had been giving me. The only things I really needed were healthcare and daycare. I did without the healthcare, but I had two children not yet in school full-time. They attended a daycare by the name of Bunny Land Pre-School, but sometimes I wasn't able to make my weekly payment by Friday. A lady by the name of Mrs. Griffin was very good to me. She was the owner's mother-in-law and would let me pay small portions of my bill until I got caught up. She told me I could get some assistance from the Welfare Department, but I told her I would manage as long as she could work with me. I didn't want anything free, just a helping hand along the way. My middle daughter began to attend school full-time within a year; my youngest daughter had about three years of daycare to go. I managed with the help of Bunny Land Preschool and the Lord. I was not always late with my payments, but I wanted to let them know how much I appreciated them. This made me try harder to have my payments on time. I made it until my youngest daughter began attending school. God was good to us, making a way when there was none I could see.

I was cleaning the house of John Brooks, a sports broadcaster, and he would do promotional advertising for different companies. Sometimes he would receive samples of whatever product he was promoting and I would work extra days in exchange for the samples. These ranged from children's clothing to furniture. By the exchange of items I was able to dress my children with some of the best clothing and had many nice, expensive items of furniture that came from furniture galleries. Mr. Brooks had a television program which aired on channel thirty-four, called, "Hello Mrs. Phillips." It was a children's program and my youngest daughter appeared on it several times, under the name "Peaches." She was able to go places and do things I couldn't afford. Mr. Brooks would also trade cleaning services for dinners out and movie passes, as well as tickets to educational places. My Heavenly Father continued to be there with us, working things out for the good.

Chapter Nine

Home Improvement Begins

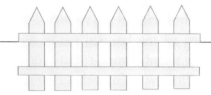

I BEGAN MAKING IMPROVEMENTS on the house. It was a full-time job in itself but well worth it. I was being my own person. I didn't have much money to buy things needed to improve the property, but God had His hand in that too! I was involved in two minor car accidents, neither of which were my fault and in both of which I sustained minor injuries. I was paid for my injuries by the other drivers' insurance companies. The money paid my bills and went toward the improvement of the house. I often said it was God's way of showing His love and blessing. I bought books to help me with the decorating of each room, trying to get my home the way I wanted it. It improved each day and I didn't get much rest because the work was continuous. I was always busy. It was as the Lord had said—I had a lot of work to do and He was there all the way with me. I worked inside and out, ashamed of where we were living. Even my brother made fun of the condition of our home. If family members were not criticizing my property, they made smart remarks like, "she won't live there long before she moves back to the east side." That was in 1981 and today, twenty years later, I have never gone back. It was a struggle, but my comfort zone had been a struggle too. I learned to handle challenges and I loved it. My depression lessened because the meaning in my life increased. I had the Lord. I was, and am, a vessel being used by Him. It took me seven years to really see great improvements in our home inside and out.

My home started out as the shabbiest house on the block. Today it is one of the best kept and decorated, with a *Better Homes & Gardens* appearance. People can't believe a single woman, with no outside help, has accomplished so much. Sometimes total strangers stop and tell me how pretty my home and yard look. Some have even parked their cars and walked up to me while I work outside, telling me it's a pleasure to drive by my home. I know it's the work of the Holy Spirit. I did almost all the work by myself with His help. I landscaped the property with my own hands, planted every living thing, big or small, and worked hard to get a perfect green lawn, front and back. Each room has an impressive, decorative touch. I designed it with love and I thank my families for giving me the opportunity to take charge of my life. They never put me down because the odds were against me and gave me the opportunity to demonstrate what a person can do if someone will give them a break.

Chapter Ten

Another Bad Relationship

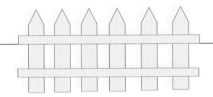

I'D FINALLY FOUND more peace in my life as well as a guy I thought would one day be my husband. I was wrong, blinded for a moment while the Father tried to tell me not to be unequally yoked. I knew things were not going to work out and tried several times to end the relationship but was too wrapped up in listening to my heart. I didn't want to be alone, but sometimes I was alone even in this relationship. It was terrible but how could I break free? I was in a trap again, not knowing what each day would bring, full of sorrow rather than happiness.

I began to cry out to the Lord again. Have mercy on me, get me out of this mess before it's too late. I am on the run again and don't know where it will end. I am getting tired of all this running, drinking, smoking. I am not able to spend time at home with my children, the home I've spent so much time preparing for us. This is not the kind of relationship I thought it would be. I deserve more than this, for the Lord had opened my eyes and showed me a better future. I am not going to settle for anything less.

After I finally left that bad relationship, the Lord spoke to me one Saturday morning. He said, "Get up and find Gay" (one of the sisters in my church). I knew His wonderful voice, when He spoke; it was so gentle and firm. I immediately jumped up and started to dress, not losing any time. My normal routine was to put on my makeup, dress, and leave home well groomed. Not this morning! God put a fire under my feet that I could not control. I had to go in a hurry to do what I was told, even though I no longer knew where my church or any of the members were, having detached myself ten years ago to become a person of the world. I didn't exactly know where to start. God helped reminded me that one of our church associates, Minister Lay, worked at the Safeway grocery store. I hurried to the store and asked her where the church was located. She didn't know exactly, but she knew the area. I was not familiar with that part of the city, so I had to ask several people along the way. Finally someone knew. I found the church, but it was Saturday and no one was there. However, the fire seemed to be quenched, so I left a note on the door asking someone to call me about their service times. I didn't really want to go but was doing what God asked of me. I had been in the world too long and didn't want to turn around.

That next morning, instead of getting up and dressing my family for church, I continued to slumber. The Lord again woke me and asked why I wasn't in church. I told Him, "Lord,

I found the church, but no one called me." This was an excuse and He knew it. He told me to get up and go to church, and I suddenly received the same fire sensation burning under my feet again. I had to hurry; there was no way I could quench this fire, and only He who had put it under my feet could take it away. I dressed my children. As soon as I entered His holy house I knew this was the calling I'd had a vision of as a child.

My relationship with God had been forgotten. I was a middle-aged woman who had been out in the world, "doing my own thing." I had a relationship with a guy to whom I was not married. Having conquered my old comfort zone, I was going to get married and then join the church so I would be able to keep him and God. That was carnal-minded thinking, not spiritual. I forgot that it was not I who had taken my security blanket away. It was not I who got the house and blessed myself with finances to improve the value of the property, making it a place of comfort. It was not I who woke me up every day, giving health and strength to make it through. I forgot because things weren't as bad as before. I put God on the back burner and took the credit.

When I entered into the church, the Spirit of the Lord was all over me. The fire was not only under my feet but all over my body. It was the most wonderful feeling I'd ever had; drugs could not compare. I knew this was where I belonged. God had told me before that I had a lot of work to do and I needed to get started. This time it was not home improvement but the work of the Lord. For the first time in my life I felt like I belonged. The missing piece of my life was finally being put in place.

I began to do whatever I could to get God's house in order, working closely with the leaders of the church and doing all I was told. My children and I started a weekly task of keeping God's house clean—we were good at that. We helped in setting up different church activities for the glory of God, an accomplishment I really enjoyed. I never missed going out drinking and smoking because I'd found the greater excitement of building a glorious relationship with Christ and the body of Christ. Because I was getting the love and protection I needed, and because I had other Christian activities to keep my mind on which brought me much enjoyment, my depression was a thing of the past. The Father was testing me to see what I would do, to see if I was learning to be faithful and obedient in all things concerning His work. I loved everything about involvement with my church and never missed any meetings. This was my family and I knew the Father was proud of me because it brought so much joy to my soul. All I ever wanted was for someone to acknowledge my presence.

One night the Father spoke to me again and gave me a vision of me teaching in a white dress. He told me what to teach on. From that night I began to sleep with pad and pencil in my bed, being ready at all times for His call. I told my pastor, Rev. Liddell, and wife, Gay, what God revealed to me and she confirmed it. From then on, each time God revealed a message to me to teach the congregation, Mother Gay and Rev. Liddell would always see to it that it would be heard. I loved to teach and do what God wanted me to do. My life changed so much I didn't miss the things of the world anymore.

However, I was smoking cigarettes and marijuana when I joined my church, reading my Bible while I was high. One day God spoke to my spirit and asked, "How can you serve me when your body is unclean? It is the temple of God." I was ashamed of myself, knowing God was right. If I was going to go all the way serving my Lord and Savior, nothing should ever take His place in me. I had found peace in Him and knew no one would ever separate me from the love of God. I was building a relationship with my Jesus, trying to learn all that was required to stay within His grace and mercy. I also knew I needed to find out more about the Holy Spirit, so that I would get the help and guidance I needed. I had tried to do it alone and failed; now it was time to try it God's way. What better way to grow than by the leading of the Holy Spirit?

Little by little I was getting more acquainted with the Him, learning to hear His voice and instructions and depending on Him for everything big or small. I love my Holy Spirit with all my heart and He knows it. There were times He would awake me with a sweet whisper and tell me things I haven't even inquired about. I always knew He was with me, that I never had to face any fear without Him. For instance, one evening I was taking a walk and the Spirit of the Lord gave me a quick warning that danger was near. I didn't know where it was coming from. My heart began racing, but I knew I had my "back-up" with me. All of the sudden, the Lord said, "Look!" and there was the terror of the neighborhood, an enormous and ferocious rottweiler which stood almost as tall as an adult. I was afraid even though I had the Holy Spirit with me and the old person within resurfaced. I looked at the dog and I looked around to see where I could run. The beast was on the loose, galloping and growling like something in a nightmare, coming my way. I stood still and frozen. In an instant, I heard the voice of the Holy Spirit saying, "Set your fear to the side," and God's Spirit said to me, "Don't run, look the enemy in the eyes and tell him to stop in the name of Jesus." Before I knew what was happening my fear had turned to anger. I stomped my foot and I told him, "No! In the name of Jesus get away from me." He stopped with a jolt as if the earth trembled, looked at me and turned. I couldn't believe how strong the power of my God was!

That was one time faith stood its ground. I believe in miracles and I will never forget the way to keep Satan and his demons from our lives. By faith believe that you have the power and authority over the enemy because of the blood of Jesus. We have to stand on it, not letting fear or anything the enemy brings our way separate us from what we believe. Satan has no authority unless we believers give it to him. It belongs to us, because Jesus paid for it with His blood. I asked that nothing I do will ever grieve my Holy Spirit; He is my comforter, my guide, and my friend. He's always in my presence. I'll never do anything without Him. I love my Heavenly Father, His Son, and His Spirit and don't ever want to be without their presence, in this life or the one to come.

Chapter Eleven

Letting Go and Holding On

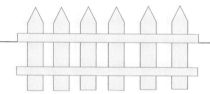

MY LIFE CHANGED. FIRST I gave up smoking. I began to deal with the bondage of cigarettes and to cleanse my body from tobacco. I didn't really like smoking but got hooked by being in the wrong company. Cigarette smoke always bothered me. Within a week I had not smoked and the cravings were almost gone. I never asked the Father to take the cigarettes. I knew He didn't want them, but He gave me the strength to give them back to the enemy. I was proud of my accomplishments and all the members of the church knew I had been freed. The regular routine after church for the smokers was to rush out into the parking lot to have that smoke, but I didn't join them anymore. God was delivering me and I wanted to be an inspiration so everyone would know that if I could stop smoking, they could too! God wanted a clean vessel to use for His glory.

Then I prayed for the strength to win another battle. No one knew about my other habit—pot smoking. God did and it was our secret. How could I tell anyone that a faithful church member, who attended all the services and taught God's Word, smoked pot? Only God and I knew what was going on and I was conquering one habit at a time. I didn't go to another source for help, just straight to the Master because I wanted to get to the core of the disease. With much prayer and faith, through the grace of God, I kicked the habit and never went to it again. This is my testimony! I felt like this particular habit kept me going; I never got up in the morning without seeking out my pot. It would give me the strength I needed to get me through the day. Pot was just another bondage that kept me tied to the enemy; it was kind of like my god. If I was ever without something to smoke, I would frantically search like a heavy dependent. If I went to bed without having something to smoke, I would be up early turning every stone to find some. It wasn't too hard to rid myself of the cigarette habit, but I did not know how I could let pot go, how I could break free. The devil will tempt us; he'll do all in his power to drag us down, kick, and beat us to keep us from God. He knows our weaknesses, the things that will tempt us to fall short. He knows when we are tired. He has no principles whatsoever, no considerations. Every child of God will be tempted. We can count it all joy, even in the face of temptation, because we are told the shield of faith is able to quench the fiery darts of the evil one (Ephesians 6:16).

We have to let go of our bondage and remember to whom we belong. It's not God's plan or will that we should be under the bondage of fear, worry, or depression. We need to let go and let God take full control of the situation. We are more than conquerors, not through our own efforts but through the Lord Jesus Christ.

I was so beaten down by Satan, I had acquired a heart palpitation due to depression. I had to seek medical advice and was eventually put on a medication for depression and another to help control my heartbeat. That helped me stay alive so I would be able to learn more about God and His purpose for me. I didn't know how to get help, but God made a way.

Did I not need Christ? Was I in control of my life? The reason I depended on pot was that it kept me relaxed so I would not do anything drastic and give credit to the enemy. The battle I was trying to win was not mine, but the Lord's! I started breaking the chain of bondage with the help of God. It was hard at first. I got rid of everything that would be involved in my marijuana habit, not wanting anything around the house to remind me of what had held me in bondage. I did not smoke around my children because I was ashamed of teaching them values that I was not applying to my own life. I did not want them caught in the circle of ignorance. My bathroom was the place I would smoke. When times got hard while I was beginning to brake the hold that Satan had on me, I would pick up my Bible, read aloud to give me strength, and let the enemy know he was not welcome anymore. I had packed his suitcase and kicked him out the door. From now on he would be under my feet where he belonged. I prayed often and God heard my cry, continually offering the Holy Spirit who gave me strength to keep going.

Day by day I was able to keep the enemy under my feet and not on my back. If you ever need a friend and a back-up, the Holy Spirit will be there and will never let you fall. Jesus said He was going away but would not leave us alone, and would send another comforter to hold our hands. We would be able to stand against any arrow the enemy shot our way. Now that's powerful!

I began to really work hard at doing God's will, becoming more and more active in the church. I was getting more confident in the provisions God had given us and was able to kick the pot habit, making me open to building a wonderful relationship with Him. I no longer had a skeleton in my closet, only love in my heart for God and all mankind. Through all this He gave me a heart of compassion for people; creed or color will never stop my love for all living things, even birds and the creatures that crawl the earth.

I got rid of my past relationship too, and even my bad acquaintances. If they didn't have godly values and act them out, they were history. Nothing would stand in the way of my relationship with the Father.

God is my husband and I don't need extra baggage. If the time comes that God sees I am ready, He will open the closed doors and send me a loving Christian husband. If not I will continue wearing the wedding ring God has placed on my finger. He will provide and I believe that. I know that Satan has no legal right to reign over anyone who accepts Christ as savior, because that man has been delivered out of his dominion and authority. He has been born into the family of God. It makes no difference how wicked a man is; if he takes Christ in as savior and confesses Him as Lord, God makes him a new creation. That man becomes the righteousness of God in

Christ. "*Therefore, if anyone is in Christ, he is a new creation; old things have passed away; behold, all things have become new*" (2 Corinthians 5:17). I am a new creation which does not need the things of the world. The righteousness of Christ is in me, and I am no longer afraid of bills, or of circumstances, or anything. The sense of lack, of guilt, of want, the consciousness of unpaid bills only fill the heart with anxiety and restlessness. The righteousness of Christ restores quietness and rest to the spirit.

Christ said, in Luke 10:19, "*in His name we shall cast out demons,*" and if we can cast out one demon, we can cast out all demons. If we have dominion over the adversary, we have dominion over all his works. Our righteousness in Christ restores our peace; it gives us the things the human heart has sought and longed for down through the ages. Our freedom in Christ is freedom from the fear of Satan and from the fear of man. We may be going through hard times, we may be suffering and there may not be much happiness in us, but there can be joy found in Christ. Happiness comes from surroundings; joy comes from a recreated heart.

I thank God each day for reaching out and taking an old sinner like me, washing, cleansing, and making me free. I ask the Lord, *Why me Lord, why me? What did I do to deserve someone like you? I am not worthy of your grace. Thank you Father.* I now know that, "*If we confess our sins, He is faithful and just to forgive us our sins and to cleanse us from all unrighteousness*" (1 John 1:9). Because of Jesus' shed blood, we are forgiven of all our sins (Ephesians 1:7). In becoming a Christian you have accepted a new standard of living which Christ called "abundant life." You begin to put off the old man and start putting on the new man (Ephesians 4:22-24). You stop doing things of the world and start doing things of God. It means dying to the old life of sin and living a new life with the resurrected Christ in control (Galatians 2:20).

After I was freed from the bondage of cigarettes, pot, and all habits that didn't include God, I was able to study His Word with a clean heart and mind without guilt. When you get God's Word in your heart, you get power in your life. Satan may come against you, but he can't defeat you unless you let him. Satan is after the word in your heart and you are no threat to him until you get God's Word in your heart. Then you become dangerous because the Word of God is the power of God. Jesus said in Mark 4:15:

> *Some people are like seed along the path, where the word is sown. As soon as they hear it, Satan comes and takes away the word that was sown in them* (NIV).

Satan is a thief. Once the Word is sown, he comes immediately to take it away, but you have to stand in faith. I have learned that the Word of God brings life and the word of Satan bring death. The Word of God produces health and the word of Satan produces sickness and disease. The Word of God brings prosperity, the word of Satan brings poverty. If you don't know how the devil operates, you'll be one of those who blames God for what the devil is doing. You need to know that God is not sending trials to teach you a lesson, and He will deliver and not destroy. In John 16:33, Jesus said, *"In the world you will have tribulation; but be of good cheer, I have overcome the world."*

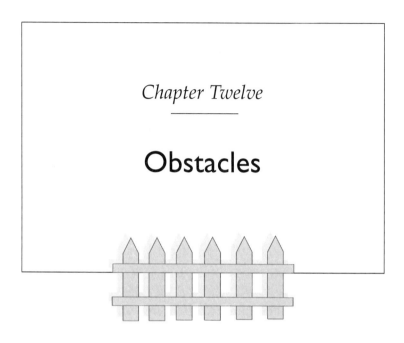

Chapter Twelve

Obstacles

WHEN I BECAME ACTIVE IN MY CHURCH, I was so happy and a lot of my stress was relieved. It felt like God had lifted a mountain from my back. My finances slowed down some and I felt it was for a reason. I attended all God's meeting at the church, but there were other problems in my life now. My children and I did not have appropriate clothing to wear and no money to buy any. I didn't know what to do, but I knew that the Heavenly Father would make a way for us. I went to different places that help those unable to buy clothing, and they would contribute items to each family member. I hated it, but at least I only had to shop for church clothing. Later, the Lord blessed me with some extra money, so I went and bought fabric and patterns to make clothes. This way we were able to attend each meeting. I really wasn't terribly concerned with where our shoes and clothing came from as long as we were able to attend church looking half decent. I think the Father wanted to test me and see what I would do. I held out because I had found something wonderful and was not going to let my pride stand in the way. God was not looking at my appearance, only my heart, so I went on and did the best I could. I had received free clothing before, but under different circumstances. They were from people I worked for who volunteered items they didn't want or need and to me. It wasn't the same. I began to wonder if I was getting ready to start charity all over again. Philippians 4:19 says, *"And my God shall supply all your need according to his riches in glory by Christ Jesus."* I wasn't to be concerned about my finances or clothing because, if this was the way I had to go about the Father's business, so be it. I needed to pray about my needs and they would be met. Jesus said:

> *...your Heavenly Father knows that you need all these things. But seek first the kingdom of God and His righteousness, and all these things shall be added unto you* (Matthew 6:32-33).

It's not a sin to be poor, but it is a sin to be proud. Satan wants you to walk by sight not by faith.

After facing this demon and putting him in his place, along came another. You always know, when you are living in Christ, the devil will tempt you. You have to submit yourself to God, resist the devil, and he will flee from you. After becoming involved in God's work at the church, there were some members that made me feel I just wasn't wanted. I felt defeated and didn't know whether I'd made the right decision to come back. I felt like I was falling into bondage again, trying to live a life in Christ and not being accepted. But God confirmed that I was where I belonged and that there are always times when it feels as though the world and half the Christians are against you. You need to realize that the only way Satan can defeat you is by deceiving you into letting go of the Word. If you will stand firm and speak forth words of faith, power, and strength, Satan has no chance and you have won the victory against him. 1 Peter 5:8 says, *"…your adversary the devil walks about like a roaring lion, seeking whom he may devour."* If you will look at him closely, you will see that Satan is a lion with no teeth. All he can do is prowl around and roar. If you fall for that roar, he's got you. *"Submit yourselves therefore to God. Resist the devil, and he will flee from you"* (James 4:7).

I did not leave the church, but stayed in prayer, seeking an answer from God and doing what He had called me to. On one occasion, after I began showing God my faithfulness, He woke me and revealed that He was going to bless me with a new car, a white one, because of my faithfulness in His service. I remember telling Him I didn't need a new car as I already had one, not knowing a time of testing was coming. To confirm His promise to me, God delivered the same message to the mother of our church several months later. I had not told anyone so the confirmation was just for me. I was often afraid to reveal the things God showed me because people would say I was fabricating it or on drugs. Some people really don't believe that God is alive, they only go to church because it's the right thing to do, it's tradition. The concept of a living God is hard to understand. We tend to believe only that He dwelled on the earth in biblical times, ignoring His presence in our present lives. Without a personal walk with God, that perspective is easy to understand. But truly, He is not dead but alive and living within our hearts. I only shared my blessings with believers. Matthew 7:6, says:

Do not give what is holy to the dogs; nor cast your pearls before swine, lest they trample them under their feet, and turn and tear you in pieces.

There are some things that should be told only to those who believe. When you are born again, God will speak to you too but you will have to believe and know that He is alive. You will have to have an ear for His voice. He speaks to us all if we will only listen. As followers of Christ, we have God's Holy Spirit who gives us understanding in spiritual matters; we also have God's Word.

Chapter Thirteen

A New Life Begins

O NE DAY WE CLOSED THE DOOR of our church and moved in with another congregation with whom we were affiliated. While we were attending Divine Guidance Church under the leadership of Bishop Randall House and wife Betty, our members continued to attend all the services provided, becoming involved as if it were our church.

One day God told me I needed to go back to school. Being stubborn I told Him I was too old at forty-five. I complained but I did what He wanted. I didn't ask what kind of school but took it upon myself to enroll at Rose State College in an introductory home interior class. This was something I wanted to do, not what God wanted me to do. After completing the twelve-week course (in which I did well), the Lord told me He wanted me to attend a school of theology to get my Bachelor's degree. Why did I not ask Him in the first place? I was starting the same pattern all over again, not realizing I was trying to take back control of my life and forgetting that God was in charge.

I began calling different theological schools to see if I could enroll in a home-study course because I wasn't financially stable enough to stop working and attend classes on campus. But God was working all the time.

One Saturday a few months later, I was lying on my sofa when the phone rang. It was a Dr. Corvin from one of the schools I'd called to inquire about my education. He asked if I would like to attend the University of Biblical Studies and I told him I was not in a financial position to do so. Dr. Corvin was persistent. He told me God had asked him to call and offer me a scholarship to get me started. I accepted. So I had my transcript transferred from Rose State to the University of Biblical Studies. In 1990 I began to take home courses with Pastor Liddell as my proctor. He give me my exams at the end of each module. After awhile I began having my neighbor give my exams. The exams were mailed to my proctor and I would then make arrangements as to the date they would be available. My grades were pretty good, and I devoted as much time as possible to my studies. I was also a single parent working full-time and paying my own tuition out of my income, so it was going really slowly. There came a time when I just couldn't continue taking money out to pay for my schooling, so I called the school and was told I could get a grant to further my education. I then began to attend classes full-time on campus and had a decision to make. Going to school full-time meant I would get a degree sooner than taking a course here and there. There were other advantages too; I could sit in on lectures and be involved with other people. I had become uncomfortable studying alone. This would be so much better, and I was feeling the anticipation of becoming a college student again.

I was still cleaning homes and a few small offices for a living which could not be managed along with full-time studies. But I had a new car which I would not be able to keep without my income. The decision was whether to drag out my education studying at home, or give up my new car so I could attend campus classes and get my degree within a few years. Without a car I'd have no transportation, so what was I going to do? I had trusted in God this far and there was no going back now. Would the Father ask something of me that I could not do? I don't think so!

Chapter Fourteen

Mastran City Bus

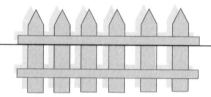

I LET GO OF MY NEW CAR, which I'd only had for a year, and began my relationship with city transportation. I'd never ridden a bus before and found out all I needed to make the transition as easy as possible. It was rough starting out. I had to ride the city bus everywhere because I didn't want to impose on anyone. Pride was still in the way and I felt like this was the purpose God intended for my life. It could break down that old spirit of pride and build up a spirit of humility. I was used to driving wherever I needed to go but all that was about to change. For several months I would cry while waiting for the bus, feeling so alone. I felt sorry for myself and asked, "Why, Lord?"

One day I was so silly. I was standing waiting for the bus and looked up and saw it coming. I was happy that my ride was there but it did not stop for me. It just kept on going. Do you know why? I was standing on the wrong side of the street! If I had thought a little more about what I was doing instead of having that wonderful pity party, I would not have missed the bus. I really began to fall into the enemy's hands. I walked and walked and cried twice as hard. Prayer was the last thing I could think of. I complained to the Lord when I should have been praying. He listened but did nothing about it. I had to learn the hard way that if you make your bed hard, you're the one that has to sleep in it.

One day I just gave up and accepted that God put me where I was for a reason. This was made clear when people on the bus would smile and hold conversations with me. I realized that I was no better than they. They too were making the best of bad situations; getting where they needed to go and blaming no one. Those pity parties were destroyers, and I decided to let God take control. He would provide for my needs. I began riding the bus everywhere—to work and to school—without shedding a tear. The Bible reveals that pride is often at the root of our stiff-necked refusal to love God or others. In the story of Adam and Eve we see that pride and stubbornness led to our first parents' disobedience of God's command. Pride cut off their physical relationship with God and led to their deaths. Mark 16:15 says, *"...Go into all the world and preach the gospel to every creature."* How could I obey this command when I was wrapped up in myself, not caring about the salvation of others? I made friends with all the people God sent my way, including bus drivers. While I was riding from one point to another I took full advantage of speaking to believers and unbelievers about God's provisions, letting them know that Christians believe Jesus is the way, the truth, and the life and that following Him brings happiness and meaning to our lives. Lack of knowledge is the main reason we allow Satan, rather than Jesus, to dominate and control our lives. Jesus is the head of the Church and the first born from the dead. He became the door, or legal entry way, into the kingdom of God. There is no other way, neither through church, nor baptism, nor paying tithes, nor good behavior. You must be born again and Jesus is the door of that new birth! Even though man is legally born on the earth, he is a child of the devil and must be reborn from spiritual death to spiritual life. The way to heaven works like this: *"...if you confess with your mouth the Lord Jesus and believe in your heart that God has raised Him from the dead, you will be saved"* (Romans 10:9). The Spirit will seal your salvation and guarantee your place in heaven (Ephesians 1:13-14).

The role of Christians in the world is to change it and raise awareness of the real meaning in life. By the quality of lives lived in response to God by word and deed, we show others their destiny and identity. We are to demonstrate what it means to be at peace and in love with the Lord Jesus Christ. We have the task of letting His light reflect off us. By living Christian lives, we can change the world.

We must seek God daily in prayer, asking that we will have hearing ears and seeing eyes. Prayer is vital to our Christian growth and maturity. God's Word reveals His will, and we must know it in order to pray effectively in agreement with it. In order to speak God's will in prayer, we have to develop a praying spirit; God will begin to speak to you, for

Jesus declared, *"My sheep hear my voice"* (John 10:27). Just as sheep learn to recognize and obey their shepherd's voice, we must learn to become acquainted with His voice and His ways. The privileged knowledge we have of Jesus Christ gives us hope that the human condition is ultimately redeemable.

To continue to grow in Christ, you will have to follow through with baptism and uniting with a church with sound doctrine. There you will find Christian friends and grow in your new life in Christ. Our families must not block our progress in spiritual matters, because nothing should get in the way of following Christ. The Holy Spirit comes to us at baptism and remains with us for a lifetime of faith and daily love for others. Through the action of the Spirit in our lives we can extend God's love to others. The weakening of our relationship with God will bring about a weakening in our relationship with others. Failure to love results in a weakening of our relationship to God. We Christians have an obligation to God, ourselves, and all mankind.

As I continued to ride the bus and minister God's Word, I always had my sword (my Bible) with me. People started recognizing me as someone who would bring comfort to the soul with God's Word. When I started using public transportation, I did not know my adventure would last six years.

Chapter Fifteen

Getting a Degree

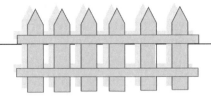

I WENT TO SCHOOL FIVE DAYS A WEEK, enjoying my professors and studying God's Word. I admired all my professors, but Professor Woodrow E. Walton stood out. I was told he was strict so it made me a little hesitant about taking his classes. After spending time with him I discovered that was completely untrue; he was the most wonderfully brilliant, highly educated professor. He did all in his power to teach me how to survive in society. I was afraid to fail some of his exams because I thought they were over my head and would give my devoted attention to his lectures in order to be prepared. He only wanted each of his students to be the best they could and it brought out his teaching skills. When I made a high grade on an exam he would rejoice with me. It made me feel special to know God was working on my behalf by sending me to someone who loved Him too, someone to steer me in the right direction and give me the self-esteem I needed! Thank you, Dr. Walton!

I appreciate all the staff of the University of Biblical Studies, but there were some who stole my heart. Ann Bellew, the school registrar, was a comfort to me and a kind, loving person, willing to help. She was a woman after God's heart. Carol Woolard was the financial aid director and, even though I was older than her, she treated me like an adopted child. She was there for me until my graduation day. Thanks Carol! Dr. Floyd Shealey, the vice-president of academic affairs, was also outstanding and very humorous. He would help me solve my schedule-planning problems. Each semester Dr. Shealey made sure I was enrolled and would be able to get to school. He kept me smiling. They were all good Christian people.

The school president was Dr. W.R. Corvin. He and his brother, Dr. R.O. Corvin, developed the concept of modular education (distance learning) that has emerged in the present-day University of Biblical Studies. The Corvin Brothers envisioned a large force of well-trained ministers who would take the gospel to the world through evangelistic and educational endeavors. They knew that many who sensed God's call to ministry would be unable to receive adequate training due to distance from the school, family circumstances, work-related pressures, or financial need. Today, the University of Biblical Studies is a degree-granting, private educational institution. Dr. Corvin is a well-educated, God-fearing man. I don't know how I would have managed without these men; they played an important part in my education. The Lord knew the best educational facility for me.

Finally, on May 17, 1997, my fifty-second birthday, I walked across the platform to receive a Bachelor of Theology certificate from Dr. W. R. Corvin. We had a very large commencement with people from all different states, all creeds and colors. My family was present as well as Gay Willis, a sister from my church. This was a wonderful occasion; I felt like God had given me wings to fly. It was glorious! I had finally put that devil under my feet and I knew he was mad. I had come a very long way with no regrets and thanked God for everything. I didn't want to go to school, but I obeyed. I was obedient to the end. After graduation, the school moved to a larger facility and changed its name to the American Bible College and Seminary, in Bethany, Oklahoma.

I can't say I ever got use to riding with Mastran. There were times I had to wait for the bus so long, I could not feel my hands or feet. I began to dress more warmly for such occasions, putting on all the clothing I would need. You couldn't depend on the bus schedule, never knowing for sure what time it would arrive. I would move around, trying to keep the blood flowing in my body so I wouldn't freeze before the bus came. When I'd look up and see it I would say, "Thank you, Jesus!" out of pure joy. I'd feel like life had suddenly sprung back into my soul. Sometimes I would pray for God to send the bus because I was so cold. Sometimes, when the snow was at least two feet deep, I'd have to walk from one destination to another to catch my next bus. People in cars often didn't respect walkers and would drive past at great speeds, splashing slushy snow all over me. When I'd see a car coming my way I would run for cover at top speed in an attempt to keep my clothing dry. If the bus didn't arrive on time I would start walking, sometimes five miles or more. I made it seem like an adventure walk, getting involved with God's creation, looking at houses, plants, and animals—anything to keep my mind off my pity party. Some days my heart was heavy with self-pity; other days I rode the bus like a champion, getting involved with the passengers, talking to them about our Lord or just listening to their problems.

The summer was another challenge, especially when the temperature was over a hundred degrees. You would need to carry an umbrella to shade your body, especially your head. You would also need a cloth to wipe perspiration from your face as well as something to drink. It is one thing to get off the bus after an eight-hour work day and walk a couple blocks to your destination. It is quite another to wander through residential areas after cleaning houses, searching for a bus stop where the bus doesn't run, and then making your way to school. After school I would need to get home. If possible, depending on the day, I would get home before the last bus stop running at six o'clock.

People who ride the bus need two thumbs up! It's hard. Even spring brought its troubles: rain, thunder, and lighting. Trying to stay dry was difficult, especially if it had rained all night. There would be deep puddles everywhere. I had conversations with strangers who felt the way I did, and tried to convince them that things would get better some day. I was easing my pain by helping someone else look at the brighter side.

My children and I also rode the bus to shop and to buy groceries. The closest store on the bus route was far away. We rarely asked anyone to take us shopping, because they would rush us or charge too much for gas. One winter day my children and I went grocery shopping on the bus. It was very cold that day; the temperature had dropped really low. One of the items we bought was a sack of greens. By the time we got home they were so frozen they began to crumble when we touched them. Sometimes we would have six bags of groceries or more and other passengers would help us put them on the bus. I have been so overloaded with bags myself, even the bus driver helped me.

I put that old pride under my feet with the one who created it—Satan. I am a living witness. Hebrews 11:1 says, *"Now faith is the substance of things hoped for, the evidence of things not seen."* I had to learn that if I held on to the promises of God, He would bring me through anything. When my faith was not as strong as it is today, I was told that what I said could bring blessings or curses. The enemy cannot read our thoughts, so I kept my mouth silent and continued day by day to stay in prayer, thinking about God's promises and His provisions.

God had promised me transportation and that He would meet my needs. I knew if I was faithful in a few things, He would bless me with more.

> *...without faith it is impossible to please Him, for he who comes to God must believe that He is, and that He is a rewarder of those who diligently seek Him* (Hebrews 11:6).

More and more each day I would try to build my faith in God, constantly seeing Him working in my life and in those around me. The stronger my faith grew, the more I knew He was everywhere. The God I serve is an awesome God. If He gave His only Son to save a person like me, what could I lose by trusting Him? I once was lost, but with God I am found. This is my living testimony.

I thought when I turned my life over to God, all my problems were over. They had, however, just begun—not the same problems, but ones that would make me stronger. My mountains were removed, but I still had pebbles to walk on. Thankfully, sometimes I had lilies to walk on too! It really pays to give your life to Christ. You don't have to fight the battles by yourself without the promise of happiness. It's a struggle out there, especially if you are caught in the enemy camp without armor. I have learned the hard way and my teacher is now the Holy Spirit who shows me how to please God and stay within His grace. I remember reading Benny Hinn's book on the Holy Spirit that woke a fire in my soul, making me want that same relationship with the Holy Spirit.

Before I gave my life to Christ, I was afraid of the Holy Spirit. I now know that God does not give us a spirit of fear but of love and a sound mind. The fear came from the enemy who knew that if I gave in to the Spirit, I would receive power from on high and give him trouble. Reading Benny Hinn's book gave me insight on the Spirit's responsibility in our lives. He can show us how to become strong Christian leaders and teachers, giving us power and helping us maintain that close relationship with God. You can't accept the Father and Son without the Spirit.

In the Bible, God never uses force. You will never read about God making people do anything. The devil and his evil spirits drive and force people, but the Holy Spirit is a gentleman who leads and guides. It is up to you to respond.

The Bible says, *"For as many as are led by the Spirit of God, these are sons of God"* (Romans 8:14). This passage uses the word "led," not "forced." The gift of God's Spirit is the secret of new life.

And I will pray the Father, and He will give you another
Helper, that He may abide with you forever—"the Spirit
of truth, whom the world cannot receive, because it nei-
ther sees Him nor knows Him; but you know Him, for He
dwells with you and will be in you... (John 14:16-17).

Knowing this about God's Spirit, I surrendered and said,
"Have your own way Lord, have your own way!" The people in
the world that are not born again cannot receive this experience
of the Holy Spirit; only born-again people can be filled with
God's Spirit. God is concerned for His children and for their
effectiveness in living Christian lives. Through His Spirit we
have courage, insight, and love in any situation.

Chapter Sixteen

Compassion for a Saint

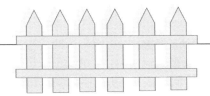

ONE DAY I WAS SITTING AT A BUS STOP downtown. There were other people standing around but no one was sitting on the bench, which had space for about four. A man who supported himself on two crutches, and had the most terrible odor you could imagine, came over to the bench. He had sores all over his head, including his ears, that were oozing a type of fluid I could not identify. The odor came from the sores. His clothing was rather dirty and in poor condition. Nevertheless, he had a nice personality and was very pleasant to talk to.

Riding city transportation, I'd become experienced with body odor, so I would carry a small bottle of perfume in my purse. When the occasion called for it, I would apply perfume under my nostrils without their knowledge. Sometimes I did this before entering the bus. If a person who needed someone to talk to had hygiene problems, I wouldn't have to act funny or try to avoid them. It was another chance to witness or just listen.

When this particular man sat down beside me, we were very close. He began to tell me war stories. One time he and his friend were on the front line. An explosion hit and decapitated his friend and, after all those years, he was never able to forget that God spared him. He shared from his past and from his small pocket-sized Bible. That day I didn't get a chance to use my perfume. I was so involved in his conversation, and in feeling sorry for him, my heart went out to him. I realized that our streets and shelters are full because of stories like his. Tragedy hits some people who are not strong enough to pull through. They wander around the rest of their days, lost, trying to forget the pain and heartache of the past. Not able to separate past from present, they can't ask for help. They don't know what to ask for or whom they can trust.

It bothered me that I was the only one sitting beside this person when there was room for others. Usually people fight to get a seat because they don't know how long they will have to wait. The people standing around were not all that well dressed, and I have seen them, on occasion, sitting with less-desirable individuals than this man.

When our bus finally arrived I got up and he scrambled to his feet. I gave him my farewell and let him know I really enjoyed our visit. I thought he was waiting for the bus too, but he looked at me with watery eyes and said, "I am not here to catch a bus." Chills went over my body. It was not what he said but how he said it. I wondered if he was an angel of God, testing me to see if the "old man" in me had died and the "new man" in Christ was alive, sharing the gift of love and compassion for all. I passed the test if that is what it was, but I think it was for me, not God. I needed to see the new person in me. The Bible says, *Be not forgetful to entertain strangers: for thereby some have entertained angel unawares* (Hebrews 13:2).

I've never had that kind of experience again but have continued talking to any and everyone about God's goodness and mercy. Riding the bus, there are people of different races, beliefs, and cultures. Everyone is a child of God. The Word says:

> *Go therefore and make disciples of all nations, baptizing them in the name of the Father and of the Son and of the Holy Spirit* (Matthew 28:19).

There is no prejudice in God's world; we are His children and He looks at the heart of the person.

Chapter Seventeen

New Form of Transportation

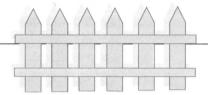

A SHORT TIME BEFORE FINISHING SCHOOL, I asked the Lord to bless me with transportation other than Mastran. *It has been six years, Lord. I have been faithful in all that I could, learning patience and replacing that old spirit of pride with the spirit of humility. I am not complaining and if it's your will for me to continue riding Mastran, I will.* I did not have enough money for car payments, but the Lord blessed me. I had just received my income tax return which did not add up to very much. There was an advertisement in the paper for a 1985 Chrysler Lebaron in bad shape on one side. It had been wrecked on the front fender and tail end and needed a hundred dollars of repair to the right front wheel. To repair it would have cost more than the value of the car. However, it ran well and I bought it for only five hundred dollars cash to which I added the repair of the wheel. That was my first vehicle in six long years. It looked bad but I didn't have to ride another bus. I thanked God every day as if it was a Mercedes! I knew the Lord would keep it running for me and never even considered mechanical problems. Any problems it ever had were minor.

I was my own person again. Another mountain had been removed by God and, although He didn't remove it when I wanted Him to, when He did I was very happy. Now I understand when people say, "He might not come when you call Him, but He is always on time, never late!" A test is an opportunity to become more persistent. God develops endurance and godly character in our lives, not defeat. When we fail in any given opportunity, we should view it as an event rather than a failure and continue trusting God and His high calling. I knew that if I was faithful with this car, God would bless me with something better when the time came. Don't give up when things look gloomy because there is a rainbow awaiting you. Once again, I was able to go places without waiting and watching for the bus. What a relief ! With your own transportation you are your own boss.

The car had neither air-conditioning nor a proper heater; sometimes the heater would blow out warm air and sometimes nothing. We would always think about how much better it was than standing outside in the cold. With the car, we would only be cold for awhile. Here again I had conquered the pride in me; there was a time in my life I would not have been caught in this run-down automobile and here we were thanking God on high for being so wonderful to us and singing, "do Lord, do Lord, oh do remember me!" We didn't get offended when people stared at us because they did not know where we'd come from. If they did, they themselves would have been rejoicing with us.

My youngest was also happy because she was working even though she was young. Before we had the car I walked with her. She would get tired having to walk to work and stand at her job, but she managed. This was a blessing to her. Our Heavenly Father does not bless us because we make demands of Him, but because He loves us.

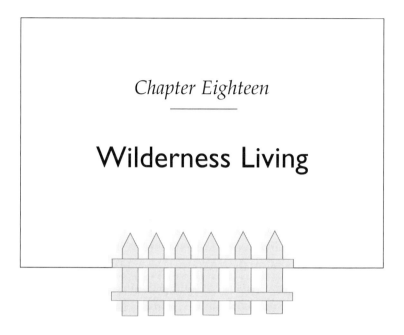

Chapter Eighteen

Wilderness Living

IN 1991, AFTER OUR CHURCH MOVED in with the Divine Guidance congregation, God took me from my church. I have been in the wilderness with God by my side, being faithful to Him. When the apostle Paul was called by God, he did not go to the synagogue to be taught by man but to the wilderness to be taught by God. I too have gone into the wilderness. My wonderful Holy Spirit is my friend, teacher, and guide. I am not saying you don't have to attend church; leave that decision to God. Church is a place in which God can use a shepherd to teach His children, where they can be together in God's presence so they won't stray. Even though I wasn't attending services at the church I continued in God's

Word day by day, hour by hour. God was always in my life. I did not go back to former things nor associate myself with people of the world, but kept myself holy and pure before God, seeking His guidance in every area of my life.

My relationship with the Holy Spirit is wonderful; I could not make it through a day without Him. I don't make any decisions without first asking Him. Believers can ask for God's help in dealing with all kinds of problems. During my wilderness time I began to reach out to God more and more, asking Him to give me wisdom, knowledge, and understanding of His Word. He was teaching me to be a spiritual, physical, and financial blessing to someone each day. He blesses givers, and I was more than happy to give. He also blessed me to be able to give words of encouragement to people caught in the devil's clutches with no way out.

The same work God had given me on the bus, I continued by telling everyone about His grace. Each day that God blessed me to see another sunrise, I thanked Him before my feet touched the floor. I would start my day by meeting God in my secret room which belong only to us. He expected me to enter into His grace. I did not need an alarm clock because the Holy Spirit would enter my room and wake me for our morning meeting. I always kept the communication open between us which is how I was able to continue living in the wilderness. The enemy would use some of his cunning devices to trick me into losing the fellowship I had with the Father. I was too strong to fall for that. I really believe the Father separated me so He could mold me into what He wanted me to be. No gates of hell shall prevail against me for I have learned to be obedient to the call of God, and no weapons formed against me shall prosper because of who I am in Christ. I dedicate all of me to the work God has called me to do. Nothing will ever separate me from the love of God; neither my family, my associates, nor demons. God plays a very important part in my life; without Him, where would I be? I dare not even think about it—it makes me shiver. The relationship I have with the Father is more precious than gold or rubies, and I never ever want to lose it. It includes the Son and the Holy Spirit. When Jesus left, He gave us the Holy Spirit for our guidance. My Jesus is now sitting on the right hand of His Father, leaving the Holy Spirit in full control until He comes back for His church, for each one of us who has accepted Jesus and lives a life in Him. This life is hard in a way but in a way it's not. You must keep your eyes on Jesus and not on the cross because He is not there. He arose the third day and now makes intersession for us.

There were times when I did not know how I was going to pay my utilities. I had cut-off notices and no money to even call and make arrangements. I would call on the Lord in prayer, saying, *Lord in your Word you say that if I will abide in you, and if your words abide in me, I can ask you for whatever I want and it shall be done unto me. Now I am asking you, in the name of Jesus, to bless me by not letting my utilities be cut off.* I tell you, I never had anything cut off. One time my gas bill was over two hundred dollars, I did not have the money, and I had a cut-off notice. I prayed really hard: *Lord, we need our gas. It's winter and we need heat. Please don't let them cut it off.* I had fifty dollars and the Lord put it in my mind to take the money to Oklahoma Natural Gas and tell them I had very little work, I was the head of my household, and when I got some money I would bring it to them. That is exactly what I did and they did not touch my gas, praise God!

In my daily walk with God I have not been sheltered from the trials of life, but given the strength to overcome them. There were times in my wilderness experience that I did not go directly to God for answers. I would pick up the telephone and call different people, asking them what to do. Then I would have several different opinions and had to determine which one to follow. That is a bad situation; one person may be a mature Christian and another just a baby. I learned the hard way to seek advice only from those who know more about the situation and can direct me properly. I went a little higher up by starting to trust God with all my heart and lean not on my own understanding. I learned patience by suffering through trials and have become a full-grown child of God.

In the past I did not have much patience to wait for the things I wanted. I would get myself into bad situations that could have been avoided. When I did have enough money to pay for what I needed, I would buy something else that really could have waited. Many times I cried and prayed that God would have mercy on me when I'd brought problems on myself. The Lord would help me out of situations when He knew I did not know any better. There were times I knew He would come to my rescue when I messed up just because I was Daddy's little girl. At other times He would let me know I needed to be more responsible. He knows what you are going to do before you do it so don't try to play innocent as if you didn't know what was wrong.

I am so happy God rescued me from the wiles of the devil. Today I could be dead or locked up in an asylum. Who knows where I would have ended up without God? Most of all I am happy for God's Spirit, my friend, my comforter, my guide.

Thank you, Holy Spirit! Jesus died to show us God's love and He rose from the dead to show God's justice and power. These events constitute God's act for our salvation; through Jesus' death we are offered life. We receive it through faith and forgiveness and the Spirit enables us to live that life on earth. Jesus helped all disadvantaged people succeed physically, financially, and spiritually. We must be obedient to God's words in order to receive these provisions. John 14:23 says:

> *Jesus answered and said to him, "If anyone loves me, he will keep My word; and My Father will love him, and We will come to him and make Our home with him...."*

God does not lie. If He made provisions for the people of the Bible, we can stand on the same provision. I am standing as long as God gives me the strength and breath in my body. I have come too far to turn around and besides, what would I turn around to? Not the same life I have rejected—my old comfort zone! That I left behind. I'll just stay here with the Lord where I will have peace and love. One day, when the time comes I will go back to my church, God will use me where He sees I am needed. I have completely surrendered my soul and body, and I have no desire for anything but to do the will of God.

We know the Church is important to God because He founded it and Christ died for it. Christianity is not an isolated experience; God means us to share it through fellowship, faith, and relationships. Partnering with others often allows us to become involved in promoting faith. The purpose of believers in the Church is to share the gospel and encourage others to find those unsearchable riches God gives to believers. This cannot be done in your own strength. We need to pray for God's guidance, and the power of the Holy Spirit to direct and empower us. We can maintain our trust in the Lord regardless of discouraging circumstances. When we have God's words in our hearts, we will be able to encourage others and convince those who do not believe. Knowing God's words also helps keep us from being lead astray by false teaching. When God called me to become a Christian, He called me to be a blessing by giving others what He has given to me. My mission as a Christian is to witness to others about saving faith. We need God's provision because we all have sinned and fallen short of His glory (Romans 3:23). God's Spirit giving me wisdom and strength made a difference when I encountered tough situations. The Holy Spirit gave me the power to overcome temptation. Satan never stops tempting you, but when you become victorious in your Christian life, he will change his tactics. To deal with these spiritual forces of evil you have to be strong in the Lord (Ephesians 6:10) and put on the armor of God (v. 11). At the same time we must hold on only to what God wills for us. By the guidance of the Holy Spirit, we can ascertain God's desire for our lives. The Holy Spirit will help us have the inner strength as well as the determination to honor God.

The godly life is not a serials of "thou shalt nots." Rather it is choosing to honor and obey by doing right and refusing to do evil. Although I wasn't active in my church, my church was still active in my heart.

Chapter Nineteen

Satan Never Gives Up!

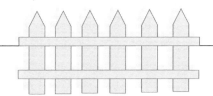

M Y PAST RELATIONSHIP CONTINUED to try and trap me, over and over. I knew God had made no provisions for acceptable sexual activity outside of marriage. All such activities violate God's plan and bring heartache, grief, and hurt. Believers who live holy, God-honoring lives will not give themselves over to passion and lust as do unbelievers who do not know God. God did not call believers to be impure, but to live holy lives (1 Thessalonians 4:7). Holy living displays the presence and likeness of Christ in believers. Holy living is one of the ways to bear witness to the world that we are indeed new persons in Jesus Christ. We spend our lives seeking happiness in things, events, and relationships. Complete satisfaction never comes, and the brief happiness those things give doesn't last long. The alternative is to seek the Lord, the One who made it all, and the joy He gives will last. Commit yourself to seeking the Lord rather than the things of the world.

We are engaged in spiritual warfare! Satan is doing all he can to defeat us and ruin our lives. He uses whatever means he can to keep people from coming to Christ for salvation. Once we are saved he does all he can to ruin our testimony and keep us from honoring Christ. We can control our own minds by our will; the Holy Spirit directs and empowers Christians to choose to guard our thoughts. The first step in avoiding any sin is to determine not to be involved in it. We need to avoid places, people (including past relationships), and things that tempt us. Pray daily so God will lead us on the path of righteousness. *I can do all things through Christ who strengthen me* (Philippians 4:13). Once I gave in to the enemy regarding my past relationship. The resulting guilt and shame were heavy on my heart and I felt like everything I had worked so hard to accomplish with the Father was completely ruined, that He would not trust me anymore. But the Bible says we have all sinned and fallen short of God's glory and I was not an exception. I prayed and asked for forgiveness, knowing what I did was wrong. Daily I walk with Him and talk with Him.

God knows our sins whether we admit to them or not. Jesus Christ died for all our sins so that when we receive Him as our savior, God forgives us, regardless of what the sin is. When believers sin, they can confess it and claim His promise of forgiveness through Christ. God's forgiveness is limitless; no sin is too great to be forgiven if we turn to Him in faith.

Now, when the enemy tries to camp at my door, I am in full armor. I let him know that I truly have a new walk, a new talk, and my life is no longer mine but the Lord's. I will not be deceived because my dependence is no longer in man. I know I have put an end to my past relationship; he doesn't show up anymore with words of persuasion. I felt like a failure when I made that mistake but, rather than give up, I used it as a stepping stone and not a stumbling block. With the Lord's help, I can overcome my failures, and I must choose the road I will take. We are all on the wide road to destruction through our sins. Eternal death in hell awaits those who remain on that road, for the Bible also says, *"the wages of sin is death…"* (Romans 6:23). You have a choice: the wide road to destruction or the narrow road to salvation. Talk to the Father on a regular basis, asking Him to guide you to His will and help you stand up for your faith daily. I know I can be strong in the Lord. I know I can face any situation and am not alone. I know I serve a mighty, wonderful God who is forgiving.

However, now that I had no relationship and no regular church activities, with what was I supposed to occupy my time? All I had was work and my family. I knew without a doubt that I would continue to put Christ first in my life, letting the Holy Spirit continue to be my friend and to teach me.

Chapter Twenty

Home Improvement Under Guidance

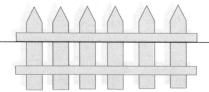

MY QUEST FOR HOME IMPROVEMENT was not in the least over. I decided to get started on my property again. I began to look at magazines and other homes in our city for decorating ideas that would work with my home. One day my daughter, Connie, and I put shutters on all the windows. They were forest green and I purchased them myself. I painted my front door—previously white—in a matching shade of green. The house had been a gray dull color but I now applied a fresh coat of white paint to brighten it up. The front of the house, which was half stucco of a faded, dirty, tan color, I painted a beige stone. I had yellow-gold awnings specially made for the two front windows and a piece across the front porch with small white trim. I also carpeted my front porch with green indoor/outdoor carpet. My daughter, Peaches, bought me a white wrought-iron glider and chair to match. I love to be creative, having lots of ideas that can't be duplicated without sewing skills. I made a cushion with two big ruffle pillows to match my awnings and sat the glider on the porch and the chair on the lawn. I even made pillows for different occasions to coordinate the wreaths on the door.

I had extra money in my house account so Mrs. Banowetz, one of the owners of the property, had her handyman take down the old shutters. They were the kind that attached to your window screen and had to be rolled open from the inside. They never did work. The screens were torn and the shutters were rainbow-colored. I went and selected storm windows of my choice. Previously I had to remove the shutters each year and put plastic over the windows to keep the ice on the outside of the window sill. My heating system wasn't helping much because there was too much cold air entering from outside. Some of the shutters were heavy because of the wooden frame around the metal. I worked at this job for about ten years because I didn't know how I could afford storm windows. I was very happy to finally get them and it sure did improve the appearance of my property. Later on that year, the McCaffrees had a beautiful, very expensive, Prestige II roof put on the house; the old roof had three, multi-colored layers and missing shingles. A central air-conditioning and heating system was installed. The one we had died one summer and we were left without cool air. Dr. McCaffree said he wanted to install a brand new system, so we wouldn't have problems for a long time.

The back fence was another embarrassment. It was an old, broken-down wire fence that people would step over to use our back yard as a short cut. We had no privacy, and I did not have much money to fix the situation. When I was just beginning to spend money wisely, I bought some fence sections and Mrs. Banowetz gave me some of the sections she was having replaced. Her handyman installed the stockade fence and that gave the privacy I needed and stopped the traffic. It was eight feet tall so it also provided security. With the backyard enclosed I was able to invest time and money in it. Mrs. Banowetz gave me items she didn't want and that really helped.

My daughter, Peaches, bought me a shed for my graduation. It was a do-it-yourself affair, which came in a flat box with instructions. Day by day I read the instructions and prayed because I knew this was going to be difficult. It turned out not to be as terrible as I thought. The Holy Spirit guided me step-by-step until one day it was completed. It was eight feet long and six feet wide. I even had to assemble the roof and apply shingles! The only thing I asked for help with was levelling the floor. This my neighbor, James, did for me. It has been standing for three years now without any problems.

While all the work was underway, I would tell my children that some days I was a man and some days a lady, depending on what challenges the day held. No one really believes I tackled the job of the shed and was successful. Now I have extra storage, mostly for my yard equipment. I love working in the yard. I have everything I need for the beautification of my garden. Before building my shed, I had a small utility room where I stored my lawn mower and equipment. I didn't have a garage.

Chapter Twenty-One

Mercy and Continued Home Beautification

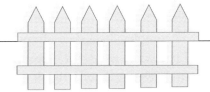

I STILL HAD THE UNSIGHTLY OLD SHED about to fall by the back door. My children and I took it apart, board by board, until it was ready to be carried away. Something happened while we were in the process of taking it apart that could have crushed me and our pet dog, if it wasn't for the grace of God. Relatively speaking, we all could have died. We didn't know what we were doing and went about it the wrong way, knocking the building down by the post that held it up. The building was about to fall and we didn't realize it wasn't going to fall the way we intended. We heard a cracking sound and almost instantly it began to collapse on us (my daughters Taunja, Connie and Peach, grandsons Kelvin and Stevie, granddaughter Tani, me and our pet dog). My daughters and grandchildren moved quickly out from under it, but I didn't move as quickly. To this day I can feel the hands of angels pulling me to safety. My feet were just a couple of inches away from the destruction. God saved my dog too! We had to get a city dumpster to discard all the lumber from the shed and it was filled to the top. It was hard pulling all those big nails from the frame that outlined the roof. We made it, but I don't ever want that job again!

I decided that this was a good place to sit lawn furniture and plants, so, with no experience, I found a pattern for an arbor over a garden. I followed the instructions as closely as possible until I had completed another adventure and painted it white. On top I laid white lattice for more shade. Some days I look out at it and wonder how I did it. People still can't believe the things I have accomplished in Christ. After the completion of the arbor, which was ten feet by thirteen feet and eight feet high, I laid green indoor/outdoor carpet on the entire area. It is especially beautiful in the summer with all my plants; God blessed me with a green thumb!

My next project was replacing the old chain-link fence that separated the front from the back as well the gate that lead to the patio. I went to Home Depot, one of my favorite spots for home improvement, where I decided on a white, French, gothic fence about four feet high. After pricing them I concluded I could assemble my own fence more reasonably. I measured the distance in the connecting boards and between each opening, bought the amount of section I needed as well as some screws, and put them together. I had some minor problems with the gate, but soon the whole thing was finished and painted. The section on the east side of the house was eight feet long and the other section, including the gate, was sixteen feet long. Another job beautifully completed by the grace of God!

I then started to build a rail fence, with French gothic posts, around my front yard for which I had to get a permit from the city-planning office. My neighbor, James, helped me dig the post holes and level them. I'd spent most of my time getting the inside of the house in order because that is where we would spend the most time. The improvement of the outside was mostly for passersby. Now, after nineteen years, my home is pretty well complete. When we moved in I did not want to let anyone know it was my house; today I have the best-looking home and property on my street. I designed my landscaping myself and people in my area often compliment me on my beautiful flowers. They are my babies.

Those who are not Christians don't understand that this work was for the glory of God and nothing would stop it. God was continually blessing me with strength, guidance, and the finances to complete the calling on my home. Some people were shocked when they found out this was my house. They would have liked to think mine was an unsightly property. Other people thought I had a lot of money based on the appearance of my home. God said He would provide for my needs. Even if the amount of money in my pocket wasn't much, He would bless me to be able to purchase whatever I needed. There is nothing impossible in Christ!

My life has oftentimes been a struggle, but when I look around and see what God has done for me, I cannot complain. I would be selfish but He would be marvelous! I could have achieved none of this without the help of God. He gave me zeal and self-esteem and His empowering Spirit. Truly, in Christ I have learned that I can do all things!

Chapter Twenty-Two

Starting a New Hobby

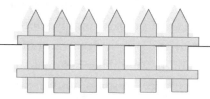

IN 1981, I ALSO DECIDED TO START A NEW HOBBY. I love Christmas so I decided to make it part of our celebration. When I moved into my home in 1981, I didn't have many outdoor decorations as I'd always lived in an apartment. I began with one small Santa, about two feet tall, and a nativity scene consisting of Mary, Joseph, and baby Jesus in a manger. I could not afford to add to my collection at that time. As the years went by I began to buy pieces after Christmas when they were on sale. As the years have passed, my collection has grown. I have been in the *Daily Oklahoman* newspaper section called the "Metro Area Light" for four years. I also was given the privilege of having a picture of my nativity scene published in the Friday newspaper—*Quail Plaza* paper—with an article about how I began decorating with a handful of items.

This recognition did not happen when I first began to decorate. For years I drove around, looking at people's displays, admiring the spirit of Christmas and the enthusiasm each person showed. Some were all about Christmas and some exhibited the love of Christ. I said to myself, *I love Jesus and I am a Christian. I would love to bring the joy of Christmas to as many people as God will send my way.* So my new-found love began, giving me something worthwhile to look forward to. I searched for something that would bring joy and happiness to each age as well as display the spiritual side of Christmas—something to bring peace and joy from the knowledge that Christ was born, died and arose so we can look forward to a new life with Him.

After all, this is only the beginning for Christians, not the end. Even though things sometimes look bleak, we can see that there is a God who loves us and gave us His best. We were never promised a rose garden, but offered eternal life so one day we will inhabit a home where the streets are paved in gold. At this place sickness and death will be no more. As a Christian I like to help give cheerfulness by letting people know there is still much joy to come. It brings joy to my spirit when I see so many people come by my house! Some take their time and just sit, while others rush by. Some even get out of their cars to make sure they miss nothing. There is a message in each scene; I decorate for children and those who never quite grew up.

Initially I prayed and asked the Lord to help me get the attention of all who travel through my small neighborhood.

Still, very few people came by. Then the Lord told me to let people know I desired their attention. So that's when I began to advertise my ability, sending out letters and pictures of my display. It worked! In any achievement you have to make yourself known; you can't wait for someone to recognize you. I decorated for about seven years without much acknowledgement

It's the same way with God. If you desire a blessing you have to be a blessing to someone else, even if it's the Lord. Praises go up and blessing come down. The more you become an asset to God, the more you become valuable to yourself. Prayer accompanied by praise will profit the desires of your heart if they are acceptable. God is the answer to prayer.

My collection has grown so much there is no room left on my front lawn. My yard is 1700 square feet! I take pride in my displays. I never really grew up as my childhood was skipped over, so I am enjoying it now instead. This opportunity gives me a chance to show God's grace in my life, and that He lives in me and in everything I do.

Chapter Twenty-Three

Our First Real Vacation

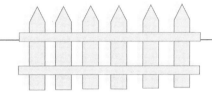

M Y FAMILY AND I HAVE NEVER had a vacation, even when the children were growing up. We would leave town for a couple days, but we never went far away. I just couldn't afford to miss work because we needed every dime. Now my children had left home except for the youngest, who was attending college. One day we were watching TV and they mentioned that contestant selection for "Wheel of Fortune" would be held in Oklahoma City, at Lowe's Home Improvement on Memorial Road. They gave the date and time, but we never saw the advertisement again. They were looking for contestants. My daughter La'Donna has always watched and admired that program, and was really good at solving the puzzles before the contestants. Of course it's a lot easier sitting at home solving the puzzles than in front of millions of people. We soon found that out. When she saw the ad, her eyes lit up and she said, "I am going down there and the Lord will bless me to get on the show." She had a very positive attitude.

When the day came for them to seek out constants, she was feeling a bit under the weather. But she said she would go regardless and we went. I thought we were wasting our time. I don't know why I was the one with negative thoughts when I have always tried to teach my children to think positively.

When we arrived, the area was taped off like a crime scene. There were many people in the parking lot—about five or six hundred and a long lineup to the mobile building where they were handing out raffle tickets with detachable stubs. A large hopper dropped off the stubs by chance, which is exactly what the "Wheel of Fortune" is. People were so excited that I began to get a fluttering in my heart. My daughter got in line and I held her son, Terrence, who was a year old. We waited until she had made it through the long line and she rushed back with her stub, consisting of numbers to be called. She was so excited I think she forgot about not feeling well. I began to get excited for her. I told her to hold the ticket and pray for what she wanted. God said that where two or more agree in prayer, He will be in their midst, and we believed Him.

We waited with anticipation until everyone received their tickets. Then the hour we were waiting for came. They announced that seventy-five people would be chosen from the large crowd that had numbers. My daughter had memorized the number on her ticket. They began to call numbers, and each time a person's number was called there was no need to repeat it. That person would come out of nowhere, running and screaming, "I got it!" The crowd was very courteous when someone came through, like when Moses parted the Red Sea. Some would pat the chosen contestant on the back as if to say, "well done." This made us even more excited. The next thing I knew, my daughter had jumped up, dropped everything in her hand, and was running through the crowd. She received the same treatment—a lot of clapping and screamed congratulations. I could not believe my eyes. For a moment I had forgotten we were the King's kids and nothing is impossible for us. I immediately began thanking God because He had heard and answered our prayer, and answered it in a hurry.

When she came back she was so full of joy. I was proud of her and began to hug and congratulate her as did everyone around us. They treated her as if she had already made a television appearance. She held in her hand a slip for another appointment at which twenty contestants would be selected from the seventy-five. These would have to audition and take selection tests. The final twenty would make an appearance on the show. She was also chosen to be one of the twenty! God is good! He doesn't get you going and then leave you to finish the race. He will be there with you until the end. The Father blessed my daughter so that we too could be blessed. Now we had to wait until we were contacted with the date of her show appearance, which was to be in California, a place we had never even been close to. The joy spread through all of our family members, acquaintances, and friends. Peach, La'Donna's nickname from birth, was like a celebrity to everyone who knew. Some thought it was a hoax, but others took our word for it and just waited to see the outcome. We were mentally ready to go when the time arrived. Only finances were a problem. Peaches was working part-time in the summer when school was out. I didn't have the money for a sudden trip, but I said I would do the best I could. We planned our getaway with other members of the family: me, Peaches, her son, Terrence, my daughter Connie and her two sons, Stevie and Cornelious, as well as my granddaughter, Tani. My grandson, Kelvin, was supposed to go but at the last minute he decided to do other things. My daughter, Taunja, and her baby, Jimmeshia, did not go either. We planned our California trip with anticipation, looking forward to the beach, sightseeing, and Peach's big win.

The day came sooner than we expected so we didn't have a chance to save much money. The Father did truly bless us because we had enough to rent a brand-new, 1999 Ford Taurus. It was very nice and plush which we needed for the long trip. We packed our suitcases and all the other accessories we thought we might need. I arranged for things to be taken care of around the house while we were away for the six days. My neighbors, Maggie and Jo Ann, were very helpful.

We were so happy to finally get away! There was no rush to get to California because we were enjoying the scenery as much as if we were going to another continent. We drove straight through, stopping only when necessary and taking turns driving as we couldn't afford to sleep in a motel. The Father blessed us with gasoline credit cards and both a Visa and a MasterCard. The credit limit wasn't high but it helped.

Finally we reached California. I was so happy to see those mountains it almost made me start screaming; they were unbelievably beautiful. We took as many pictures as we could. We got a room at the Holiday Inn Express in Culver

City, close to the studio. Even though we did not have much cash on hand, we did not care. God would make a way. We went to the beach and played in the sand and ocean, taking advantage of the sightseeing even though we were strangers in a brand new city. God was in our midst.

People drove so fast, I was nervous on the road. The speed limit is obsolete to them and they don't obey traffic signs. I began to drive like them so we would not get hit or killed. Other drivers would honk at me something crazy just for obeying the speed limit.

The next day we went to the MGM studio in Culver City so Peach could make her appearance on national television. She arrived early that morning, and when it was time for them to call each contestant to the platform, she ended up being the last one. They pulled numbers to know who would air each time. By this time she was so afraid and tired, she just wanted to get it over with. Connie and I were just as nervous, especially when she didn't call the right letters. She started to get some money on the board until one person took full control of the game and no one won anything but him. He came out a big winner. Peaches didn't win any money on the program, but the opportunity to appear on national television spend time in California was enough. She did receive cash and some consolation prizes for her appearance. I was happy to see that tiring day end.

Peaches was disappointed that her expectations were not fulfilled. She thought God was going to bless us with lots of money and a new car. We left the studio and hurried back to the hotel to undress and rest. We all were disappointed in her loss, but we did not let that stop our vacation. When the time came for us to go home we were ready and tired, looking forward to telling our friends and relatives all about the trip God had blessed us with.

We now knew how to plan family trips: how to set a date that would be appropriate for everyone, how to decide on a place, save money for a rental vehicle, and prepare ahead.

Chapter Twenty-Four

Work of the Ministering Spirits

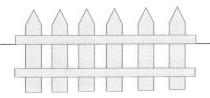

I N Psalm 91:11-12 it says:

> *For He shall give His angels charge over you, To keep you in all your ways. In their hands they shall bear you up, Lest you dash your foot against a stone.*

Ministering spirits have been beneficial to me in my walk with God. One time I was hired by Taunja's landlord to paint some trim on her house and the double garage door. I liked to paint and needed the money. Her landlord supplied everything I needed to complete the job. I had been painting hard, trying to complete the job so that I could get paid because I had a bill that was past due. As I was working on the eaves of the house the ladder moved and, before I could catch myself, I went straight down. It was so sudden the only thing I could feel was a sort of smooth gliding motion. I knew afterward that angels had held me so I didn't experience the full impact of the fall. I was about ten feet up and fell onto concrete.

The only injury I thought I sustained from the accident was a sprained toe. There were no bruises and no great pain except for that little toe which got caught in the ladder on the way down. After the fall I had the whole neighborhood at my daughter's house because they thought I needed an ambulance. I was so embarrassed I wanted to disappear, not thinking to check myself for bodily injuries.

After I regained my composure, I still had a small area to complete. Everyone tried to talk me into stopping but, being hard-headed, I finished. I hopped around on that sprained toe for three months and it never healed. My children finally talked me into going to the doctor because sometimes the pain was very intense. At the emergency room the doctor took an x-ray and found out it was broken. If it had not been for ministering spirits, I could have broken many bones or even died. My Heavenly Father gave them charge over me and they held me in their hands, keeping me from harm. Daniel 3:28 says:

> ...Blessed be the God of Shadrach, Meshach, and Abed-Nego, who sent His Angel and delivered His servants who trusted in Him, and they have frustrated the king's word, and yielded their bodies, that they should not serve nor worship any god except their own God!

In another incident, my daughter Connie and I were carrying a section of my shed that I had put together. We were bringing it outside and I was walking backwards. I stumbled and fell and the weight of the lumber landed on me. My body hit the pavement with great force, but, again, I did not feel the impact of fall. It felt as if my whole body was held in midair as I floated, feather-like, to the ground. My daughter could not believe her eyes, and we began to thank Jesus and His ministering spirits. I was just speechless. God said He would send His angels and deliver those that trust in Him and I am a trusting servant.

One morning I was warming the car. I usually take my second set of keys out of my purse and lock my purse in the car so I won't have much to carry. This morning I forgot and locked both sets in the car. My daughter was too far away to come home with her keys so I had a couple of guys try and open the door with a clothes hanger. This went on for about an hour with no success. I called my neighbor, James, to see if he had a slim jim since he was a mechanic. When he arrived with the device and tried it for about thirty minutes, we still had no success. Finally, the Lord brought my ministering spirits to my attention because they are for supernatural help in time of need. I looked at James who is also a Christian and said, "Ministering spirits, will you please unlock this door so James and I can go to work, in Jesus name?" Within a couple seconds the lock popped up, even though he was using the same tactics he'd been using for thirty minutes.

The Bible speaks a great deal about angels and how they minister in our lives. Angels are also used to help God's people when help is needed. They also help us every day in our struggle against the enemy, through the will of God.

After the devil had tempted Jesus in the wilderness without success, the ministering spirits came and ministered to Him (Matthew 4:11). I learned to use what God has given me in my times of trouble and that angels protect my home, my family, and me, wherever we go. I take not only Jesus and the Holy Spirit, but also my angels. They even protect us while we are asleep. I am never without protection and I know to take full advantage of what God has given me. God's covenant and His loving contract with His people is that He is always faithful to us. He will never fail to be responsible for the children He created in His image and likeness. In response to His love, God asks that we renew our fidelity to Him by obeying His loving will. He desires that we love Him back, and, in return, we will receive the desires of our hearts.

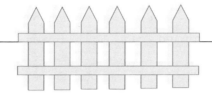

Chapter Twenty-Five

Provisions in My Life

THE HOUSE WASN'T IN MY NAME UNTIL 1998, even with all the hard work I had put into it. Late in 1998, Dr.'s Robert and Mary Anne McCaffree did the most wonderful thing ever; they had my home refinanced and put it in my name through their bank. Without them there was no way I could have made the transaction because of my credit standing. But God was still working on my behalf. Several thoughtful people told me they would not invest money and years of work into a property without ownership. I told them that as long as the McCaffrees had anything to do with the property, I would have nothing to worry about. And I didn't! God had them in the plan for my life from the day I entered a verbal contract with them to be their housekeeper. I respect and love them and have ended up being more than just a housekeeper; they are my family. Through all the years they have never disappointed me. Thank you Doc and Mary Anne and my babies, Sarah and Matthew. God was in the plan, He was with me, and I knew He was with them too. They only wanted the best for me and my children and were there for me even when I wasn't there for myself. They believed in me and I knew I could trust them. I raised two of my children working for the McCaffrees. After Peaches was first born I went back to work and she would lie on their bed while I cleaned. When my kids were old enough they would play and swim with Sarah and Matt. We were never strangers to the McCaffree family.

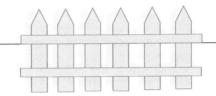

Chapter Twenty-Six

Life Must Go On

WE CAN'T DO ANYTHING ABOUT THE PAST, but we can change the future. My biggest problem was that I did not know who Alice was or where was she going or what she would do when she got there. How could I love anyone if I didn't know myself? I had a hunger in me that I could not satisfy and for a long time did not know I was searching after something only God could give. When I accepted Christ as my savior it was the beginning of real life.

Being born again means entering a new family—the family of God. You are delivered from the kingdom of darkness and translated into the kingdom of Jesus (1 Corinthians 1:13). All Christians belong to one body and Jesus is the head (1

Corinthians 12:13). Our body is His Church (1 Colossians 1:14-19). You need to be a member of a local church that believes the Word of God and exalts Jesus as the way to salvation (Acts 4:12). When you accept Jesus as your Lord, you assume some new responsibilities. You must trust in, surrender to, and rely upon Him as master, ruler, and leader of life. Before receiving Christ you were your own master, making all decisions according to your wisdom and emotions. Now you allow Him, moment by moment, to control your new life.

We cannot be in Christ and have the devil's nature; either we are in the family of God or in the family of Satan. There can be no real development of faith, no strong victorious Christian life, with mixed conceptions. We are either new creations or we are not. I have learned that if I am to maintain any kind of faithful walk, I must put down my carnal nature and let the love of God work within my spirit. In order for me to walk in faith I have to walk in love; without love my confessions don't mean a lot to God. To have perfect faith and to receive answers to prayer, you have to learn to walk in love.

The pleasures I once sought have lost their taste and attraction because being a Christian is an incomparable privilege. God chose us because He has a task for us to perform. The fact that He has chosen us does not make us better than anyone else. It does, however, give us special responsibilities. Jesus needs us in His Church to continue His work of healing and loving. To love as Jesus did is a challenge and a great responsibility.

Chapter Twenty-Seven

The Testimony I Live By

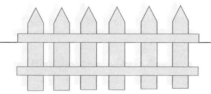

T HIS IS MY TESTIMONY. If the Lord can do this for me, He can do the same and more for you. He loves us all and if you take one step toward Him, He will walk you out of any situation. Don't give up; you are something in the eyes of God. Be persistent and don't let poverty, sickness, or anything else cause you to give up. No matter how bad things appear or how hopeless a situation might seem, God will triumph and vindicate those who trust Him. We must completely depend on His support to help us persevere. God expects committed Christians to face trying circumstances with patience. Even bad things can be beneficial if we will surrender to God and commit our lives totally to His use.

I am the person I am today because God delivered me from the shackles of my comfort zone. The outcome of every situation depends on whether you permit your problems to defeat you or allow them to be used for the glory of God. I could not have done it by myself, but when I made an honest effort, God was there to help me. When I prayed, I asked God to take care of my family and the things in our life we could not bear, to give me the strength to be a good provider and a good parent. He then began to carry me through all the storms and difficulties. We are to face suffering with patience. With God's help we can endure any situation. God bless you! Don't give up! *But as for me and my house we will serve the Lord* (Joshua 24:15).

See Luke 15 for the story of a lost man who was found.

Our Comfort Zone in 1981

Our Comfort Zone today